The Language
of **Cybersecurity**

Compiled and Edited by
Maria Antonieta Flores

**The Content
Wrangler**
Content Strategy Series

The Language of Cybersecurity

Credits

Series Producer:	Scott Abel
Copy Editor:	Trey DeGrassi
Series Cover Designer:	Marc Posch
Publishing Advisor:	Don Day
Publisher:	Richard Hamilton

Disclaimer

Trademarks

XML Press
Laguna Hills, California
http://xmlpress.net

First Edition
ISBN: 978-1-937434-62-5 (print)
ISBN: 978-1-937434-63-2 (ebook)

This book is dedicated to my daughter Shalewa and grandson Akinsheye who make the world more beautiful through their art and to my fellow systems engineers and technical communicators who through their art make it easier for technical and not-so-technical people to understand each other.

Table of Contents

Table of Contents

Foreword

Speak in such a way that others love to listen to you.
Listen in such a way that others like to speak to you.

—Unknown Author

Language: It is the basis for how we communicate, how we coordinate, and how we find common ground. It is also the basis for conflict and confusion. And that is why a common understanding of terminology matters. Tonie Flores and the dozens of subject matter experts who contributed to this book know the realities of the language of cybersecurity. In this book, the contributors define 52 terms that every business professional should not only know but also be able to communicate clearly to the organizations they support.

One definition that is not contained in the defined terms, but which all professionals need to live up to, is *accountability*.

We need to realize: 1) who we are accountable to, and 2) what we are accountable for.

Digital transformations are embedding technology into the fabric of our lives. Typically, these technologies are meant to help or assist us, but one key element is often overlooked: exploits that take advantage of technological vulnerabilities will increasingly affect the well-being of almost everyone in our society.

Therefore, it is incumbent upon all of us to properly shape the way we design, develop, and implement digital transformations to best manage and mitigate information security, privacy, and other risks, while still challenging ourselves to create technology that helps people. This is what we need to be accountable to.

The World Economic Forum 2017 Global Risk Report[1] listed "cyber dependence" in its top five risk trends, just below climate change and polarization of societies. It also indicated that "…technology is a source of disruption and polarization." I believe technology is a tremendous opportunity for economic and societal benefit. I believe that technology can connect and enrich people's lives – if done correctly and for the right reasons.

---

[1] http://reports.weforum.org/global-risks-2017

If we carelessly implement technology in order to chase opportunities or simply prove that we can, we won't be successful in realizing the digital transformations that can change lives and protect people. Instead, we will be setting ourselves up for a digital disaster. By focusing on the opportunities along with our obligations to implement them in the right way, we can achieve digital transformation and digital safety to ensure tomorrow is better than today for everyone.

So, ultimately, not only information security professionals but also business professionals are accountable to the organizations they support, the customers they serve, and society. And they are accountable for making sure we achieve digital transformation and digital safety.

Malcolm Harkins
Chief Security and Trust Officer
Cylance Corporation

Preface

The RIGHT perspective makes the impossible POSSIBLE
—Unknown Author

It's a matter of perspective. *The Language of Cybersecurity* tackles a communication gap in cybersecurity.

As a technical communicator, I have been explaining technology to the not-so-technically inclined for decades – not the innards and workings, just what they need to get their work done. To them, technology is a set of tools to improve the productivity, quality, and joy that they get from their work. I make that possible and easy.

The Language of Cybersecurity came about when I was researching for a *PCI DSS* procedure documentation project. I have written user procedures in dozens of realms. I had the confidence to take on this one, but I needed a little domain knowledge and context. It was a challenge to find general information at the very high level that I needed to do the work. There were glossaries, Wikipedia, and many blog posts and articles to read, but nothing I found defined the subject with just enough context to point me in a useful direction.

This book intends to help to fill that gap. It presents a set of cybersecurity terms that every business professional should know – a first level of context for the uninitiated. Each term has a definition, a statement of why it is important, and an essay that describes why business professionals should know the term. Many of the essays use metaphors or examples that help you to apply what you already know to understanding the cybersecurity term and its use.

This book is not exhaustive. It highlights 52 terms that are useful to know whether you are confused by a report from your IT professionals, contemplating working in a security environment, or just need to present security matters to others in understandable terms. In addition, there is a glossary of additional terms and a set of references to give you further information about the term.

The contributors to this book are thought leaders, educators, experts, regulators, bloggers, and everyday practitioners who work in their own way to communicate important security information. They share my desire to make these important concepts accurate and accessible.

Most people know more about cybersecurity today than they did last year. I started this book to hasten the time when we can talk about cybersecurity with the same fluency that we have when we talk about other complex technical things, such as automobiles or cell phones. We might not know how to build them or exactly how they work, but we can sure use them.

The content is divided into digestible chunks of related terms:
1. **Vulnerabilities:** weaknesses that can threaten your information
2. **Exploits:** methods used to attack your systems and information
3. **Defenses:** steps you can take to safeguard your information
4. **Planning, Management, and Controls:** tools that you can put in place to mitigate security risks
5. **Compliance:** rules of the road for cybersecurity

The Language of Cybersecurity is both an easy read and a handy reference for business professionals and cybersecurity specialists.

A note on the term cybersecurity: Over the last several years, this term has been spelled in several different ways, including cyber security, cyber-security, and cybersecurity along with variations in capitalization. We chose to consistently spell the term as cybersecurity, because this form is now preferred by the Merriam-Webster dictionary and the Associated Press (AP) style guide. Although common usage does vary in different countries – for example, you may be more likely to see Cyber Security in the UK – we decided to stick with one form for this book, unless the term appears differently in a company name or the title of a publication.

Acknowledgments

This book wouldn't have been possible without the 52 contributors, who put up with changing deadlines, delays, and changes in focus. Thanks to all of you.

In addition to the 52 experts whose definitions and essays make up the bulk of this book, I would like to thank the additional contributors who helped craft the introductions to each chapter and the glossary.

The contributors to the glossary are: Debra Baker, Luis Brown, Christopher Carfi, Dennis Charlebois, Frank DiPiazza, Steve Gibson, Chris Gida, James McQuiggan, Michael Melone, Michael Moorman, Taylor Stafford, and Kathy Stershic. The contributors to the introductions are: Phil Burton (exploits), Jessica Fernandez (vulnerabilities), Guy Helmer (defenses), and Matt Kelly (compliance). You can find biographies for these contributors in *Additional Contributors*.

Behind the scenes, the following people made important contributions to this book:

- Scott Abel, Rahel Anne Bailie, Trey DeGrassi, John Diamant, and John Elliott, who reviewed all or significant portions of this book.
- Trey DeGrassi, who copy edited the book, and Richard Hamilton, our publisher.
- My go-to cybersecurity subject matter experts: Debra Baker, Mel Johnson, Justin Orcutt, James McQuiggan, and Keyaan Williams, who generously shared their cybersecurity knowledge and their contact lists.
- My coach Mira Wooten who helped me win my battle with writer's block.
- My STC-Berkeley buddies Susan Becker, Mysti Berry, Nicki Davis, Clarence Cromwell, Joe Devney, Rebecca Firestone, Richard Mateosian, and Joy Montgomery, for professional support and suggestions.
- My Sunday writing group, Kathy Andrews, Sheila Baisley, LD Louis, Gerald Green, Ted Terrific Marsh, and BevieJean Miles who helped me to find my authentic voice and convinced me that my voice has an audience.
- My Vision Masters Toastmasters club members who were always a willing and encouraging audience for my experimental explanations of things too technical for everyday humans to care about.
- My friends and family who kept me bathed in love, well wishes, and positive vibes.

Vulnerabilities

All systems have weaknesses – places where a determined attacker has the potential to breach security and either disrupt your organization or steal your data. Therefore, cybersecurity planning requires a solid understanding of the places where your systems, processes, and staff are vulnerable to attack.

The single weakest part of any system is the people who use it. People are vulnerable to a wide range of exploits, including *social engineering* attacks such as *phishing*, which attempt to fool people into revealing passwords or other sensitive information, to *insider threats*, where employees take advantage of their position to breach security.

According to the threat management experts at Cofense, phishing has increased dramatically over the last several years, with 91% of breaches initiated by phishing[92]. The reason for this increase is that phishing is effective. Although organizations can reduce their risks through defenses such as *multi-factor authentication* and *behavioral monitoring*, human vulnerabilities remain the weakest link in cybersecurity.

You can reduce your exposure to human vulnerabilities through *security awareness* programs and by creating a strong security culture, but you cannot eliminate human vulnerabilities.

Weaknesses in computer software, such as *zero-day vulnerabilities*, are another means malicious hackers use to breach security. The WannaCry *ransomware* attack combined a human vulnerability (a phishing message to get readers to click on a link) with a software vulnerability (a software bug in Microsoft Windows) to gain access to systems, encrypt data, and demand a ransom to recover the encrypted data[108].

You can reduce your vulnerability to such attacks by keeping your software up to date and keeping your systems backed up. If you develop software, you should employ practices such as *static application security testing (SAST)* to reduce the likelihood that you will introduce vulnerabilities in your software.

However, humans are prone to error, regardless of the extent to which you mount defenses. And because humans write computer programs, computer software is prone to errors. No matter what defenses you implement, you cannot eliminate all risk. Therefore, in addition to finding vulnerabilities and mounting defenses, you need plan for how you will respond to and recover from a cybersecurity event. This includes creating *incident response plans* and *business continuity plans*.

The terms in this section provide a starting place for understanding the wide range of vulnerabilities that business professionals must deal with.

Terms in this section:

- Social Engineering
- Security Fatigue
- Shadow Security
- Data Leak
- Insider Threat
- Zero-day Vulnerability
- Dark Web

David Shipley
Social Engineering

What is it?

A human-centric manipulation technique that uses deceptive tactics to trigger emotionally driven actions that are in the interests of a cybercriminal or attacker.

Why is it important?

Exploiting people can be an effective means for criminals to bypass security processes and technology controls. Social engineering can be used to create a point of entry into a computing device, application, or network via an unsuspecting person.

About David Shipley

David Shipley is a recognized Canadian leader in cybersecurity, frequently appearing in local, regional, and national media and speaking at public and private events across North America. He is a Certified Information Security Manager (CISM) and holds a bachelor of arts in information and communications studies as well as a master of business administration from the University of New Brunswick (UNB).

David helped lead the multi-year effort to transform UNB's approach to cybersecurity. He led UNB's threat intelligence, cybersecurity awareness, and incident response practices. His experience in managing awareness programs, risk management, and incident response helped shape the vision for the Beauceron platform.

Email	david@beauceronsecurity.com
Website	beauceronsecurity.com
LinkedIn	linkedin.com/in/dbshipley

Why does a business professional need to know this?

Social engineering attacks can cost millions of dollars. Recently, MacEwan University was the victim of a phishing attack[135] that fooled employees into changing banking information for a major vendor. As a result, nearly $12 million was transferred to the attackers.

Social engineering can take many forms. It includes phone scams, face-to-face manipulation and deception, email-based phishing attacks, targeted *spear phishing* of specific individuals, and whaling attacks, which are aimed at senior executives. Social engineering poses a tangible business risk for security professionals, executives, and boards of directors alike.

Social engineering through phishing is a growing threat to individuals and organizations of all types. According to the 2016 Verizon Data Breach Investigations Report[136], 30 percent of targeted individuals will open a phishing email message, with 12 percent also opening attachments or URLs which may contain malicious code.

Over the past two years, a new type of social engineering attack targeting senior executives and financial departments has emerged. Known as *whaling* (because "big fish" are the targets), these attacks seek to deceive employees to authorize six, seven, and even eight-figure fraudulent wire transfers.

Countering social engineering requires organizations to think beyond technology-based defenses such as email filtering, *firewalls*, or *endpoint* detection. An effective technique to defend against social engineering is to identify and manage employees at risk and create an educated workforce that is aware of all forms of social engineering.

Engaging leadership and employees in managing the risks of succumbing to social engineering attacks can be an effective proactive strategy. Further, this creates a critical cultural shift from cybersecurity as an IT-centric service to cybersecurity as a shared responsibility.

Mary Frances Theofanos
Security Fatigue

What is it?
The psychological state one reaches when security decisions become too numerous and/or too complex, thus inhibiting good security practices.

Why is it important?
Security fatigue can cause weariness, hopelessness, frustration, and devaluation, all of which can result in poor security practices.

About Mary Frances Theofanos
Mary Theofanos is a computer scientist with the National Institute of Standards and Technology, Materials Measurement Laboratory, where she performs research on usability and human factors of systems. Mary is the principal architect of the Usability and Security Program, evaluating the human factors and usability of cybersecurity and biometric systems. She represents NIST on the ISO JTC1 SC7 TAG and is co-convener of Working Group 28 on the usability of software systems.

Email   mary.theofanos@nist.gov
Website   nist.gov/topics/cybersecurity

Why does a business professional need to know this?

Security fatigue — feeling tired, turned off, or overwhelmed in response to online security — makes users more likely to ignore security advice and engage in online behaviors that put them at risk. Users favor following practices that make things easier and less complicated, even if they recognize that these practices may not be as secure.

Security fatigue presents a significant challenge to efforts to promote online security and online privacy. The ability to make decisions is a finite resource. Security fatigue is a cost that users experience when bombarded with security messages, advice, and demands for compliance.

Too often, individuals are inundated with security choices and asked to make more security decisions than they are able to process. Adopting security advice is an ongoing cost that users continue to experience. When faced with this fatigue and ongoing security cost, users fall back on heuristics and cognitive biases such as the following:

- Avoiding unnecessary decisions
- Choosing the easiest available option
- Making decisions driven by immediate motivations
- Choosing to use a simplified algorithm
- Behaving impulsively
- Resignation

Understanding how the public thinks about and approaches cybersecurity provides us with a better understanding of how to help users be more secure in their online interactions. The following steps can help users adopt more secure online practices:

- Limit the decisions users have to make for security
- Make it easy for users to do the right thing related to security
- Provide consistency (whenever possible) in the decisions users need to make

Iacovos Kirlappos
Shadow Security

What is it?
Security measures that staff create to manage security to the best of their knowledge and ability, avoiding official security policies and mechanisms that get in the way of their tasks and reduce productivity.

Why is it important?
Shadow security practices reflect the best compromise staff can find between getting their job done and managing the risks to the assets they use. It presents an opportunity for the organization to learn how to maintain both security and productivity.

About Iacovos Kirlappos
Iacovos Kirlappos is an information security and risk professional with strong academic and industry credentials. He obtained his bachelor of arts in computer science from the University of Cambridge, UK, and his master of science in human-computer interaction, master of research in security science, and PhD in information security from University College London.

Email	iacovos.kirlappos@gmail.com
Twitter	@ikirlappos
LinkedIn	linkedin.com/in/iacovos-kirlappos-phd-89477b18

Why does a business professional need to know this?

Shadow security emerges in organizations where: (1) employees have reasons to comply with security and are motivated to do so, but (2) security mechanisms are not fit to support their work goals. As a result: (3) a significant amount of security mediation takes place at the team level, and (4) employees become isolated from the security division.

Although not compliant with official policy and sometimes not as secure as employees think, shadow security practices reflect a working compromise between security and getting the job done. Its occurrence signals the presence of unusable security mechanisms. These can lead to errors and workarounds that create vulnerabilities, people ignoring security advice, and systemic non-compliance, all of which can act as noise that makes genuine cybersecurity attacks hard to detect in systems.

Security management should not ignore shadow security. Organizations must be able to recognize when, where, and how shadow security practices are created. Once identified they should not be treated as a problem, but rather as an opportunity to identify shortfalls in current security implementations that can be leveraged to provide more effective security solutions.

This can be done by taking the following steps:

- Simplifying compliance with security
- Measuring the effectiveness of security mechanisms after deployment
- Engaging users when designing security solutions
- Leveraging the position of team managers as both a mediator for security and a conduit, providing feedback as to the appropriateness of security solutions in supporting productive tasks
- Giving team managers the responsibility of acting as mediators for security and as a conduit for feedback from users on the impact of security processes on productivity

Dennis Leber
Data Leak

What is it?
A loss of information from your systems that could harm your business or customers.

Why is it important?
Data leakage is important to cybersecurity and business professionals because of the negative impact to finances and reputation that losing critical information can have on an organization. Data ownership spans a business at every level of leadership, and protecting data is a business responsibility that must be reflected in every organization's goals.

About Dennis Leber
Dennis Leber is an information security executive with over 10 years experience in IS/IT management and over 20 years of management experience across various industries. Currently, Dennis serves as the chief information security officer (CISO) at the Cabinet for Health and Family Services for the commonwealth of Kentucky, where he works to protect over 400 in-house applications and associated data. Dennis has also worked in the automotive industry, healthcare, federal government, and military to protect data and the systems that house them.

Email	mostinterestingmaninis@gmail.com
Website	mostinterestingmaninis.com
Twitter	@dennisleber
LinkedIn	linkedin.com/in/dennisleber

Why does a business professional need to know this?

Understanding data leakage means knowing what data is important, where sensitive data resides, and what could cause data to improperly leak outside your organization. It is also important to understand that a leak can be intentional or unintentional, and the impact of a leak can be rated as low or high.

Understanding data leakage enables you to work with cybersecurity specialists to develop controls to protect sensitive information and reduce this risk to your business. The potential impact of data leakage is not limited to just your systems or one specific information medium. Recent examples, such as the Equifax breach[38], highlight the potential for serious consequences, including legal actions, loss of jobs, and damage to business reputation.

Other examples of significant data leaks include the following:

- Personal details for more than 198 million US voters were left on a publicly accessible server by a company working for the Republican National Committee(RNC)[39].
- Personal information, including billing addresses and details of financial transactions, for 4 million Time Warner Cable subscribers was left on an Amazon cloud server with no password[40].
- A spreadsheet containing private notes about more than 30,000 customers at a restaurant frequented by celebrities was accidentally attached to a broadly distributed email message[41].
- An Iranian hacker stole 1.5 terabytes of data from HBO, including scripts, unaired episodes of several HBO programs, and technical data about HBO's network, including passwords[42][43].
- A Verizon vendor accidentally left information about 6 million Verizon subscribers on a cloud server for more than a week[44].

These examples, which are just the most notable of many that have occurred over the last few years, make it clear that data leaks can cause serious damage to an organization's reputation and bottom line.

Thomas Carey
Insider Threat

What is it?

A hostile action against an organization performed accidentally or maliciously by individual(s) who possess intimate knowledge of, and access to, a company's infrastructure, security, and business processes.

Why is it important?

The term is important because insider threat is one of the main causes of data *exfiltration* – theft of data – affecting organizations today. Insider threats can cause grave damage to an organization's finances and reputation.

About Thomas Carey

Thomas Carey has over 12 years' experience in information security practices, with a strong knowledge of both government and corporate security requirements. He currently works with Science Applications International Corporation (SAIC) as a chief software systems engineer. He holds the following certifications: Certified Information Systems Security Professional (CISSP), Certified Information Security Manager (CISM), and Security+. He has experience in database administration, system administration, cloud, and virtualization technologies.

Email	thomascareyjr@gmail.com
Twitter	@doctomtomx2
LinkedIn	linkedin.com/in/thomascareyjr

Why does a business professional need to know this?

As organizations try to gain application and infrastructure efficiencies with cloud and virtualization technologies, they are flattening the network, eliminating system silos, and connecting systems company-wide. This has led to more and more people having broad, privileged access to company data and resources.

With increased access comes a greater potential for abuse, both malicious and accidental. Business professionals must ensure that proper security controls are in place to ensure that permissions are used appropriately.

Two critical security controls are training and employee monitoring:

- A robust security training and threat awareness program helps reduce the success of *phishing* and *social engineering* attacks by helping employees learn how to avoid accidentally releasing privileged user information to outside malicious actors.
- *Behavioral monitoring* software can track employee behavior on the network and detect actions that appear to be unauthorized, suspicious, or malicious. Such software can often prevent such activity in real time, by logging questionable activities and notifying the appropriate stakeholders of suspicious employee actions[64].

Insiders have different motivations, including financial, competitive, nationalist, or even simply a desire to cause mischief or chaos. Verizon's *Data Breach Digest* describes a variety of case studies, including one where an insider stole more than 500,000 British pounds by manipulating a banking system to redirect money to offshore accounts[65].

James McQuiggan
Zero-day Vulnerability

What is it?
A product vulnerability that the developers are unaware of.

Why is it important?
Zero-day vulnerabilities are important because there is the potential for them to be exploited before developers have a chance to patch the affected product. Once a zero-day vulnerability has been detected, companies often have very little time to correct the issue before the vulnerability is used to attack the product.

About James McQuiggan
James R. McQuiggan, Certified Information Systems Security Professional (CISSP), is a cybersecurity expert in the central Florida area who works as a product and solutions security officer for the Siemens Wind Service Americas company. James is the president of the (ISC)^2 Central Florida, supporting cybersecurity professionals in education and training.

Email james@iphotographit.com
Twitter @james_mcquiggan
LinkedIn linkedin.com/in/jmcquiggan

Why does a business professional need to know this?

Imagine that you have discovered a secret way to get into your office that no one else knows about and that allows you to enter without going through your normal security sign in. You always use the front door to go to work, because you don't want people to know about the secret entrance. Now imagine it's after hours, and you've forgotten something at work. Signing in at the front desk, badging in, getting your item, and signing out is too much of a hassle. So you decide to use that secret way to get into the office, get to your desk, and collect your forgotten item without ever disturbing the security guard.

This essentially is how a zero-day exploit works. It uses a vulnerability that is unknown to the owner to get into a product. Using a zero-day vulnerability, an attacker can gain access or take control of a system without the user ever knowing about it.

The product is vulnerable to exploit from the day the vulnerability is discovered – the zero day – until the owner creates and distributes a patch to fix the problem. Even after a patch has been created, the product will remain vulnerable until users apply the patch to their copies of the product. Therefore, it is important for users to apply patches as soon as they become available to minimize the amount of time their systems are exposed to the threat.

One proactive measure for software developers is to use *threat modeling* and other techniques to reduce the number and severity of as yet undis-covered zero-day vulnerabilities in the first place. One strong measure for security professionals is to conduct a *vulnerability assessment* and create an *incident response plan* and a *business continuity plan* for their company.

In 2016, zero-day vulnerabilities and exploits were in the news because a group that calls itself The Shadow Brokers released alleged US National Security Agency (NSA) zero-day exploits, including EternalBlue, which was used to create the WannaCry and Petya exploits[151].

Chris Vickery
Dark Web

What is it?

A part of the internet that is intentionally hidden from standard browsers. It is accessible only through specialized software with an appropriate configuration or authorization. The dark web – sometimes called *darknet* – provides anonymous access to the internet for people who want to keep information about themselves hidden from view. It also provides anonymous hosting.

Why is it important?

Although the dark web is primarily known to the general public as a place where illegal activity takes place, its original intent was to provide a private environment. Any business that has a need for anonymous browsing or anonymous communication may find the dark web useful. Business professionals also need to know about the dark web because it is used for illegal activities, including storage of stolen information.

About Chris Vickery

Chris Vickery is a cybersecurity expert cited by The New York Times, Forbes, Reuters, BBC, LA Times, Washington Post, and many other publications. He has assisted the Motion Picture Association of America (MPAA), Thomson Reuters, Microsoft, Citrix, AARP, Verizon, and dozens of other entities in plugging serious data breaches affecting hundreds of millions of individuals. Chris has assisted investigations conducted by the Federal Trade Commission (FTC), the Federal Bureau of Investigation (FBI), the Texas Attorney General's Office, the US Secret Service, the US Department of Health and Human Services (HHS), and the State of Kansas.

Email	cvickery@kromtech.com
Website	mackeeper.com
Twitter	@VickerySec
LinkedIn	linkedin.com/in/chris-vickery-b0664412a

Why does a business professional need to know this?

The dark web was designed for enhanced end-user privacy that is purposefully hidden from conventional search engines. It is traditionally accessible only through special software – such as *Tor* or *I2P* – that uses a technique called *onion routing* to preserve anonymity.

In the past, the dark web was primarily of interest to cybersecurity specialists, but increasingly, business professionals are finding it necessary to understand the dark web and to work with cybersecurity specialists to evaluate the risks and opportunities it poses. The dark web is infamous as a digital marketplace where illegal transactions occur, such as the sale of drugs, weapons, child pornography, malware, and stolen personal information such as credit card and social security numbers.

However, it is also used for legitimate, private transactions or communications. For example, the news organization ProPublica has a site on the dark web that can be accessed anonymously, enabling anonymous sources to privately and securely submit news tips[36].

Business professionals should also make sure that their cybersecurity specialists have the skills needed to check common dark web markets for any mention of their company and discover if any private company information is for sale.

There is a lot of misinformation associated with the dark web, both in the form of uninformed gossip as well as conspiracy theories. As with the internet itself (called *clearnet* to differentiate it from the rest of the internet), astute users question everything.

Exploits

Yankees in Georgia! How did they ever get in?
—Margaret Mitchell, *Gone with the Wind*

An exploit is both the *malware* that uses a vulnerability to successfully violate security objectives and the act of violating security objectives. Hackers write exploits designed to steal login credentials or create a backdoor to install additional exploits onto a user's system.

Exploits can be carried out by many different people and entities, including the following:

- Criminal gangs, data-mining companies, and political organizations, who use exploits for financial or political gain.
- Government intelligence and police agencies, who use exploits to collect information about a user's browsing habits, online postings, and written documents.
- Terrorist groups, who use exploits to attack critical infrastructure such as power plants.

Exploits attack a vulnerability with the intention of disrupting a system, gaining privileged access, or stealing information. To gain access to a system, exploits such as *phishing*, target human vulnerabilities, while exploits such as *zero day* and *buffer overflow attacks* target technological vulnerabilities. Here are some types of exploits:

- *Zero day*
- *Watering hole attack*
- *Phishing*
- *Spear phishing*

Some of the highest profile security breaches, including the hacking of email messages from the Democratic National Committee (DNC) during the 2016 elections in the US, have happened because users were fooled by a *spear phishing* attack – an attack that uses a personalized email message to lure a reader into revealing login information or clicking on a link to malware. Once the hackers gained access to the DNC system, they were able to install tools that allowed them to retrieve email messages and other data[137].

The terms in this section are critical to understanding the means by which attackers attempt to compromise security, which in turn will help you mount effective defenses.

Terms in this section:

- Phishing
- Ransomware
- Botnet
- Advanced Persistent Threat (APT)
- Buffer Overflow Attack

Jeffrey Rogers
Phishing

What is it?

An exploit in which an attacker, typically using email, attempts to trick a computer user into opening web links, entering personal information into a web form or fake website, or taking an action that allows the attacker to obtain sensitive information. Spear phishing targets a specific individual or group of individuals using personal information.

Why is it important?

Phishing and spear phishing are the most common attack methods for attackers to gain an initial foothold into an organization or obtain sensitive data.

About Jeffrey Rogers

Jeffrey Rogers has over 20 years of IT security experience and holds Certified Information Systems Security Professional (CISSP), Certified Information Systems Auditor (CISA), Security+, and EC-Council Certified Hacking and Forensic (CHFI) certifications. As vice president of the Customer Success and Technical Operations Group, Jeffrey is responsible for overseeing and growing Cofense's customer support and client success teams. Previously, Jeffrey served as PhishMe's senior client engagement manager, where he worked alongside customers to develop and manage unique phishing awareness programs. Jeffrey holds a master's degree in information security assurance from Capitol College and a bachelor's degree in finance from the University of Kentucky.

Email	Jeffrey.Rogers@cofense.com
Twitter	@vangoghz
LinkedIn	linkedin.com/in/vangoghz
Facebook	facebook.com/phishme

Why does a business professional need to know this?

Email phishing is one of the most popular methods used by cybercriminals to trick users into taking actions that install *ransomware* onto their computing devices. In the first quarter of 2016, the cybersecurity researchers at PhishMe Research determined that ransomware accounts for 50% of all phishing email messages.

As of the end of March 2015, 93% of all phishing emails analyzed contained ransomware[94]. In the first quarter of 2016, the number of phishing emails hit 6.3 million, a 789% increase over the last quarter of 2015[92]. Subsequent studies from PhishMe and other researchers continue to show the same trends.

With all the technical and administrative controls in place today, our cyberattacks are still growing at an alarming rate:

- 91% of breaches start with spear phishing
- Average time to identify a breach, 146 days
- Average time to contain a breach, 82 days
- The global average cost of a data breach, $4 Million[92]

Business professionals looking for a defense must familiarize themselves with the emotional triggers that persuade and convince users to interact with phishing messages.

These emotional triggers can be:

- The promise of a reward for interacting
- The appearance that the message comes from a respected person, such as a family member or a boss
- An appeal to curiosity

Phishing email attacks usually ask the recipient to click a link, enter data in a form, or open an attachment.

Because humans are the first line of defense against cybercriminals, we must educate our customers and co-workers so they can recognize malicious phishing attempts and report them to the appropriate authority.

Dave Kartchner
Ransomware

What is it?
Malicious code that encrypts files on a computing device, enabling an attacker to demand a ransom from the legitimate owner to recover the encrypted data.

Why is it important?
Numerous high-profile ransomware cases – including the May 2017 WannaCry ransomware attack that struck at least 50 organizations[108] – have occurred over the last several years, involving medical centers, police departments, and government organizations. These occurrences show the negative impact ransomware can have on an organization's operations and finances.

About Dave Kartchner
Dave Kartchner has been a cybersecurity professional for more than 15 years both in private industry and with the US Army Reserve. He has an extensive background in computer forensics and incident response, including threat hunting, threat intelligence, penetration testing, and security operations. He holds undergraduate and graduate degrees from Brigham Young University and Boston University. He currently works as a senior computer forensic engineer at Silicon Valley Bank in Santa Clara, CA.

Email   dkartchner.ca@gmail.com
LinkedIn   linkedin.com/in/cyberwarrior

Why does a business professional need to know this?

Symantec's 2017 Internet Security Threat Report[109] notes, "During 2016, ransomware was one of the most significant threats facing both individuals and organizations." Another disturbing trend noted in this report is that the average ransom amount continues to trend upwards with a 266% increase between 2015 (US$294) and 2016 (US$1,077).

Both Symantec's report and Verizon's 2017 Data Breach Investigations Report[111] predict a continued upward trend in ransomware attacks, their sophistication, and the amount of ransom demanded. Thus, the ransomware threat is not fading away anytime soon.

The potential impact of a successful ransomware attack is enormous for any organization that depends on digital/electronic data or systems to conduct business.

To reduce the risk of a ransomware attack, organizations should consider best practice defenses such as the following:

- Data *backup* and restore processes
- *Business continuity* and *disaster recovery* plans that include ransomware scenarios
- An *incident response plan* for ransomware

These best practices can help lessen the negative consequences on operations and revenue that a successful ransomware attack can generate. Business professionals must communicate with decision makers in the organization regarding the risks and consequences of a ransomware attack on the organization.

Tolu Onireti
Botnet

What is it?

A network of computers that have been infected by a malicious software program – a bot – which turns them into *zombie* machines that can be remotely controlled by an attacker without the zombie machine owner's knowledge.

Why is it important?

Cyber criminals use botnets, which can contain from 100 to over 100,000 zombies, as free resources to execute attacks. A botnet can execute *Distributed Denial of Service (DDoS)* attacks, store illegal content, and send spam, viruses, phishing email, and spyware.

About Tolu Onireti

Tolu Onireti is a cybersecurity consultant. She has more than 10 years of cybersecurity experience in secure development lifecycles, management, and implementation of cybersecurity programs. She holds a master of science in telecommunication engineering and a bachelor of science in electrical and electronics engineering. Tolu has also worked at Cisco Systems, IBM, and Solutionary (NTT Security). She holds Certified Information Systems Security Professional (CISSP), Project Management Professional (PMP), and CompTIA Security+ certifications.

Email	Tonireti@gmail.com
Twitter	@tolutop
LinkedIn	linkedin.com/in/tolu-onireti-pmp-cissp-comptia-security-a835644

Why does a business professional need to know this?

Cyberattacks using botnets are on the rise. On October 21, 2016, top internet websites were not accessible for most of the day due to a *Distributed Denial of Service (DDoS)* attack caused by the Mirai botnet[18]. The Mirai botnet attacked the managed domain name server (DNS) infrastructure of the internet infrastructure firm Dyn. The attack stopped after it was mitigated by Dyn's engineering and operations team. Dyn estimated there were at least 100,000 Mirai zombies used in the attack.

A computer can be infected by a bot when an end user clicks on a link or opens an attachment that contains the bot. Another method of infection is when a bot exploits a vulnerability in the computer software.

Zombie machines are controlled by a cybercriminal called a bot-master or a bot-herder. The bot-master sends instructions to the zombies through a command-and-control center.

A cybercriminal can use a botnet in many ways, including the following:

- To launch large-scale DDoS attacks, rendering the target unavailable until the cyber criminal stops the attack or traffic to the target is sanitized and normal operations restored
- To store illegal content on zombie computers
- To steal data such as credit card numbers, bank credentials, and other sensitive information from zombie machines
- To send *spam*, *viruses*, *phishing* email, and *spyware*
- To execute *click fraud*, by repeatedly clicking on ads to generate fraudulent hits

Possible symptoms of a bot infection include: slow internet connection, low system performance, system crash, or mysterious messages. *Antivirus* software can often detect the existence of a bot, remove it, and restore normal operations.

To prevent computers tablets, smartphones, and other devices from being infected by a bot (or any malicious software), install an antivirus program, educate end users of the risk associated with clicking on URL links or opening attachments from untrusted sources, install patches as soon as they are released, and setup the system to automatically install updates.

Paul Brager, Jr.
Advanced Persistent Threat

What is it?

A form of malware whose purpose is not to damage an environment, but rather to persist undetected and harvest data such as intellectual property or customer data.

Why is it important?

Advanced persistent threats are significant because they represent a different modus operandi for hackers, where persistence is key to the operation of the malware, and the objective is data theft.

About Paul Brager, Jr.

Paul Brager, Jr., M.Sci, Certified Information Systems Security Professional (CISSP), Global Industrial Cyber Security Professional (GICSP), Certified Information Security Manager (CISM), has been a contributing member of the cybersecurity community for over 20 years, specializing in security architecture, industrial cybersecurity, and digital forensics and incident response. He has extensive experience in the oil and gas, manufacturing, chemical, and telecommunications sectors, having held various leadership roles throughout his career.

Email	professorbrager@outlook.com
Website	hiddencyberfigures.com
Twitter	@ProfBrager
LinkedIn	linkedin.com/in/professorbrager

Why does a business professional need to know this?

Advanced persistent threats (APT) are dangerous because they can remain undetected while harvesting critical customer or intellectual property data from the target organization. Depending on the type of data harvested, a company can suffer significant damage to its reputation and be exposed to serious legal consequences.

Most APTs are delivered by *social-engineering* mechanisms, such as targeted campaigns or *spear phishing* against an organization. Once a system has been compromised, the APT seeks not only to persist, but to discover, proliferate, elevate privileges, and remain undetected.

The ultimate goal is to extract targeted information from the victim in a manner that is difficult to detect by ordinary detection and *incident response* methods, generally using encryption to blend in as ordinary *HTTPS* traffic.

An APT can persist for months or, in extreme cases, years without detection, sending data to its command and control structure only when a certain set of criteria are met.

APTs have evolved into more malicious types of malware, such as remote access *trojans* (RAT) and, potentially more devastating, various forms of *ransomware*. At the root of each of these advanced forms of APT you can still find the original elements of APT: increased levels of encryption for command and control, malware that is aware of sandboxes and other containment technologies, and better subversion techniques. These elements have made APTs the current method of choice for cybercriminals.

Business professionals should ensure that their cybersecurity specialists understand and employ the tactics, techniques, and procedures required to detect these exploits[1].

Shawn Connelly
Buffer Overflow Attack

What is it?

An attack that targets the buffer memory of a device or program by sending more data than the program can handle, thereby writing the extra data into a nearby memory location, which could allow an attacker to run a piece of malicious code.

Why is it important?

If software is not properly patched or designed with secure coding principles from the start, these types of malicious attacks can cause great harm by allowing programs or external parties to access protected nodes or information.

About Shawn Connelly

Shawn Connelly holds two master's degrees, one in cybersecurity and information assurance and another in IT management. He holds his Certified Information Systems Security Professional (CISSP), Certified Chief Information Security Officer (CCISO), Certified Ethical Hacker (CEH), Computer Hacking Forensic Investigator (CHFI), Cisco Certified Network Professional (CCNP), VMware Certified Professional (VCP), VCP-NSX, and six Microsoft Certified Solutions Expert (MCSE) certifications. Shawn has worked for more than 20 years in IT, including the last five years as a director of security.

Email	shawnconnelly1@gmail.com
Twitter	@VirtualizationG
LinkedIn	linkedin.com/in/virtualizationg

Why does a business professional need to know this?

A buffer overflow can be explained by the old adage that you can't put 10 pounds of potatoes in a 5-pound bag. When too much data is written to a block, it can overwrite adjacent memory leading to data corruption. A program or device can crash or an attacker can insert malicious code into the overwritten memory and try to execute it.

Because buffer overflow attacks exploit weaknesses in the design of hardware or firmware, defending against such attacks must begin in the early design stages of product development. Because such attacks can potentially give attackers the ability to gain administrator privileges, damage databases, or steal data, mitigating the threat of buffer overflow attacks should have a high priority.

Correctly patching devices, including updating firmware on network equipment, is essential to protect against these types of attacks. When developing products, your best defense is to follow industry best practices for design, development, testing, and code review. Reviewing a program or website for security vulnerabilities before it is placed into production may take a few extra steps, but it will save money if it prevents your system from being exploited. An ounce of prevention is worth a gallon of protection.

A simple buffer overflow attack can take down a web page, a database server, a content management system, or a mail server. The recent Meltdown and Spectre vulnerabilities have shown that buffer overflow attacks have the potential to open up systems to devastating attacks[20][21]. These vulnerabilities have been identified in processors manufactured by Intel, AMD, and ARM, which are in a considerable number of computers and devices, including phones, tablets, laptops, and servers.

Defenses

Cyberattacks can come from software, hardware, and people. Business professionals must defend against attacks from all of these sources. It is no accident that this is the largest section of this book. You are not helpless against cyberattacks. There are things you can do throughout the business lifecycle to help protect your digital assets.

The best defense includes multiple, layered security measures that build each layer as if the others did not exist. For example, you should implement *authentication* as if your *firewall* has been breached. Don't assume that the firewall is 100% effective in keeping attackers out.

Thinking about the path by which an attacker can breach your systems' security gives insight into how you can prevent, or at least detect, an attack. An *attack vector* is the manner in which an attacker attempts to violate the security of a system, for example by exercising flaws in the system or tricking authorized users into assisting in the attack.

Your first line of defense is to understand your environment, including computer systems, websites, software, and other technology and evaluate the risks and ease of attack posed by the various vectors. If a particular attack vector has a high risk and can be easily exploited, then preventative measures such as mitigating controls are urgently needed.

On the other hand, if an attack vector is low risk or is impossible to exploit – perhaps due to existing *controls* – preventative measures may be less urgent, or it may be sufficient to simply monitor those systems for exploit attempts.

If an attack vector involves tricking authorized users, then protections such as user training, *multi-factor authentication*, or *behavioral monitoring* may be helpful.

It makes sense that so many of the terms in this section have to do with users. The most important defense for software users is to keep your systems up-to-date with the latest *patches* and carefully monitor security settings. The following figure shows some of the other defenses related to users:

Defense – Users

Awareness Training

security awareness
situational awareness
behavioral monitoring

Identity Management

identity management
authentication
multi-factor authentication
biometrics
non-repudiation

The following figure shows some of the defenses related to technology:

Defense – Technology

Software Creators

encryption
sandboxing
firewall
hardening

Software Users

privilege
endpoint security
physical access control

The terms in this section cover a wide range of defenses that you can mount against both human and technological threats.

Terms in this section:

- Authentication
- Endpoint Security
- Multi-factor Authentication
- Identity Management
- Physical Access Control
- Biometrics
- Security Awareness
- Situational Awareness
- Behavioral Monitoring
- Non-repudiation
- Privilege
- Firewall
- Encryption
- Sandboxing
- Hardening

Neal Fuerst
Authentication

What is it?
The implementation of policies, practices, and technology to enable positive identification of people, devices, and applications.

Why is it important?
Understanding authentication is critical for establishing a secure environment because you must reliably know the identity of the people, devices, and applications accessing your resources in order to properly govern access and permissions.

About Neal Fuerst
Neal Fuerst is a detail-oriented, highly technical computer security expert with nearly 30 years of experience working in information security. An effective project manager with significant experience leading complex technical teams, he has taught various topics ranging from public-key infrastructure to electronic evidence processing and computer forensics.

Email	nfuerst@cygnacom.com
Website	cygnacom.com
LinkedIn	linkedin.com/in/neal-fuerst-a40411

Why does a business professional need to know this?

Authentication lies at the core of cybersecurity. As business professionals, we constantly refer to our user community and the applications and resources they access. However, we often overlook the details of how we prove who our users are. If we don't know who our users are, or we don't have confidence in the process used to vet their identities, then how can we determine the appropriate level of access?

Authentication is a combination of policies, practices, and technology:

- **Policies:** a set of principles adopted by an organization to guide decisions and practices. Proper cybersecurity policies mandate that all users, devices, and applications shall be positively authenticated in order to access or share resources. In addition, depending on the environment, policies may mandate a particular authentication level of assurance. Level of assurance refers to how much confidence you have that the identity provided by the user, device, or application is true. That is, how strong is the binding between the asserted identity and the true identity?
- **Practices:** the methods used regularly to carry out activities. Often, best practices of an organization are documented, becoming formal policies. As business professionals, we need to ensure that our practices support reliable authentication.
- **Technology:** in this context, the software and hardware used to implement a particular authentication method. Depending on your policies, you may need to implement enhanced authentication techniques such as *multi-factor authentication*, which provide higher levels of assurance.

Many organizations now allow employees and visitors to access company networks using their own devices. Companies must be able to properly authenticate users and their devices, regardless of whether the devices are company-provided or employee-owned. To safely make such a shift, your authentication methods must account for every user, application, and device that accesses your infrastructure.

Michael Dombo
Endpoint Security

What is it?

A subset of cybersecurity that protects networked devices, such as smartphones and medical equipment, that are usually accessed by an individual user or group.

Why is it important?

Endpoints are a vulnerable point of entry for breaches. Because of the large number of connected devices available and the wide diversity of types, endpoints are difficult to manage and keep vulnerabilities patched.

About Michael Dombo

Mike Dombo is the founder and president of the Kensington Sales Group. With twenty-five years of sales and marketing experience, he helps emerging technologies in the cybersecurity vertical reach their buyers. Mike is a premier sponsor and member of the board of directors for the Cyber Association of Maryland, Inc.

Email	mike@kensingtonsalesgroup.com
Website	kensingtonsalesgroup.com
LinkedIn	linkedin.com/in/mike-dombo-8766835

Why does a business professional need to know this?

Endpoint security provides the first line of defense against malware being introduced into a network. Proper endpoint vulnerability management reduces the available *attack surface* and helps keep the entire network secure.

Business professionals need to know about endpoint security because they often manage one or more endpoints (laptops, tablets, phones, etc.). Therefore, they are responsible for ensuring the following:

- Device software and firmware is up to date
- Devices are protected with passwords or other secure controls
- Devices are regularly backed up
- Devices are regularly scanned for *viruses* and *malware*

Cybersecurity specialists need to understand endpoint security in relation to other forms of security such as network or application security. Proper endpoint configuration and access control policies should hamper an intruder's ability to traverse a network and gain access to more sensitive data or to obtain escalated network privileges. Specialists should also ensure that security measures are easy to follow and do not put an undue burden on users.

Endpoints can potentially move from one physical location to another and possibly access less secure networks such as airport or hotel wifi networks. As a result, endpoint security that travels with a device provides the first line of defense against malware being introduced into the network. Endpoint security is most effective when integrated with other forms of security.

Dovell Bonnett
Multi-factor Authentication

What is it?

A combination of two or more dissimilar *authentication* modes, called factors (possession, knowledge, inherence, location, or habit), that must be presented as part of the process of authenticating the identity of a person or device requesting access.

Why is it important?

When properly implemented, multi-factor authentication (MFA) makes it harder for someone to impersonate an authorized user, giving you a higher level of confidence about the identity of a person or entity attempting to access your system.

About Dovell Bonnett

Dovell Bonnett has been creating computer security solutions for over 20 years. In 2005, he founded Access Smart to provide cyber-access control solutions to government and small-to-medium-sized businesses in areas such as healthcare. His premier product, Power LogOn, is a multi-factor authentication, enterprise password manager.

Dovell is a frequent speaker and consultant on the topic of passwords, cybersecurity, and multi-factor authentication. His most recent book is *Making Passwords Secure: How to Fix the Weakest Link in Cybersecurity.*

Email	Dovell@access-smart.com
Website	access-smart.com
Twitter	@AccessSmart
LinkedIn	linkedin.com/in/accesssmart
Facebook	facebook.com/AccessSmart

Why does a business professional need to know this?

Many data breaches start with the theft of user credentials. At the 2017 Black Hat Conference, a survey question asked: Which of the following is most responsible for security breaches? The choices were: humans, not enough security software, unpatched software, or other. Eighty-five percent (85%) of the hackers surveyed said humans.[81]

When the same group was asked what was the strongest barrier to stealing credentials, sixty-eight percent (68%) said it was the combination of multi-factor authentication and data encryption.

Business professionals need to know about multi-factor authentication so they can adapt authentication to meet their needs while balancing expense with security.

Authentication factors include the following:

- *Physical* controls such as key cards
- *Biometric* factors such as fingerprints/iris scans
- Two-step authentication such as a code sent to a mobile device

MFA happens when a combination of two or more of these methods is presented at the same time. What makes MFA more secure than single-factor authentication is that the odds of a hacker possessing two or more of the authentication factors at the same time are very low.

One factor alone is weak authentication. Cards can be cloned, passwords cracked, biometrics fooled, and smartphones stolen. The combination of two or more of the same factor (like two cards, two passwords, or two biometrics) is not true multi-factor authentication. While stronger than having only a single factor, combining two of the same factor is double single-factor authentication.

The first step to hacking into many networks is to bypass the logon authentication by stealing a legitimate user credential. Cybersecurity starts by first knowing who is knocking on the virtual front door. That knowing begins with multi-factor authentication.

Evelyn de Souza
Identity Management

What is it?

The information security discipline that establishes and manages the roles and access privileges of individual users, including humans and machines, within a computer network. Identity management is also known as identity and access management.

Why is it important?

Identity management enables companies to control who, how, when, and which users access information or digital assets. Identity management systems can enhance productivity in addition to protecting assets.

About Evelyn de Souza

Evelyn de Souza is an advisor to privacy and data security startups and the Cloud Security Alliance. She consults with organizations across the technology spectrum. Evelyn was recognized by CloudNOW as one of the Top 10 Women in Cloud and in 2015 as a Silicon Valley Business Journal Woman of Influence.

Email	e_desouza@yahoo.com
Website	cloudtweaks.com/author/evelyn
Twitter	@e_desouza
LinkedIn	linkedin.com/in/evelynd

Why does a business professional need to know this?

Business professionals need to understand identity management because it is at the center of controlling access to digital assets. Access control requires you to authenticate the identity of people and computers. Identity management systems also help ensure that each user has only the privileges required for the job at hand and no more.

In today's digital world, identity management is evolving. One important trend is federated identity management, which enables users to leverage the same user name and password across multiple networks. Single sign-on (SSO) is a similar capability that, again, allows users to use the same credentials across different systems.

In addition to interoperability across platforms and networks, there are schemes that leverage attributes of an individual's identity other than user names and passwords. One example of such a scheme is *biometrics*, which refers to the use of human characteristics such as fingerprints for access control.

Successful identity management programs are clearly planned and aligned with the organization's goals, and they weigh risks against potential business gains. After decades of planning, organizations are finally getting closer to having effective online identities that improve security.

Chris Wynn
Physical Access Control

What is it?
The ability to control entry to physical locations based on factors such as date, time, and access level. Access control systems can also create audit trails, raise alarms, and adjust authorizations based on the threat level.

Why is it important?
Access control helps ensure that only authorized people have access to your facilities.

About Chris Wynn
Chris Wynn is a security director in Southern California. His background in law enforcement and school district security contributes to his ability to provide sound security advice and best practice recommendations. Mr. Wynn writes for a variety of security magazines and is a frequent speaker at safety conferences on the topics of electronic access control and video surveillance.

Email	chriskwynn@gmail.com
Twitter	@cwynn289
LinkedIn	linkedin.com/in/chriskwynn

Why does a business professional need to know this?

Business professionals need to understand the capabilities of current access control systems, which go well beyond traditional lock-and-key controls. Electronic access control systems allow facility managers to control who has access to each point of entry in a facility and when they have access. Such systems can generate reports that show when and by whom an entry point was accessed and whether access was granted.

In the event of a threat, such as an active shooter or unauthorized intruder, an access control system can make it possible to immediately secure a facility, regardless of whether security staff is on site or not.

Electronic access control systems rely on credentials that identify a particular person. Credentials can include physical objects such as a key card, personal knowledge such as access codes, or *biometric* measures such as a retina scan, facial recognition, or a fingerprint.

In a key-based system, lost keys are a constant security concern because when a key goes missing, the only way to ensure site security and safety is to re-key all affected locks. This can be very expensive if the missing key is a master that has access to multiple locks on site. With an access control system, you simply revoke access for the lost credential and issue a new credential with the same access rights, potentially saving thousands of dollars in labor and materials.

Stephen Simchak
Biometrics

What is it?

A means by which a person can be uniquely identified by analyzing distinguishing traits such as fingerprints, retina and iris patterns, voice signatures, gait, and facial characteristics.

Why is it important?

Biometrics-based security is increasingly being used to identify people – for example, using a fingerprint to unlock a smartphone. Security professionals are turning to biometrics both for convenience and because password-based security is not secure enough. Inherent traits, such as a retina pattern or gait, cannot be easily counterfeited, making them potentially more secure, especially when used as an additional factor in a *multi-factor authentication* scheme.

About Stephen Simchak

Stephen Simchak has been defining, measuring, analyzing, and improving existing business processes for over 15 years. His knowledge, skills, and abilities have made people, processes, and projects more efficient, effective, quality-focused, and secure.

Stephen is a certified Project Management Professional (PMP), Six Sigma Green Belt, and Microsoft Certified Solutions Expert (MCSE) in addition to holding Network+ and Information Technology Infrastructure Library (ITIL) credentials. He has worked with the US Federal Aviation Administration (FAA), General Electric, National Institutes of Health (NIH), Phillip Morris USA, and the US Department of Veterans Affairs.

Email	simchaks@gmail.com
Website	infusionpoints.com
LinkedIn	linkedin.com/in/sweetsteve

Why does a business professional need to know this?

Password-based security requires users to enter a string of characters to gain access. This security scheme can be bypassed by nefarious parties without much effort. An unauthorized user could guess a common password, e.g., 123456 or QWERTY; a hacker could trick a user into disclosing a password through a phishing attack; or an unauthorized user could use software tools to crack or guess a complex password.

Biometrics-based security relies on physical or behavioral characteristics, which are difficult to circumvent without an inordinate amount of effort. An unauthorized user cannot guess what a user's biometric data looks like or recreate it without tremendous effort. The effort required to mislead a user into providing biometric data, capturing that data, and recreating it, currently outweighs the benefits of using the data.

Biometric-based security often captures data in a template and stores it in a database. If this database is not properly secured, the data can be stolen. In 2015, the United States Office of Personnel Management (OPM) announced that its security had been breached and 5.6 million sets of fingerprints were stolen[12][13][14]. This is worrisome because a person's retina pattern or fingerprints cannot be reset like a compromised password. As with any other security technique, biometrics depends on the confidentiality, integrity, and availability of the underlying data.

Biometrics and passwords can be utilized together for two-factor authentication (2FA), where something a user knows (e.g., a password) can be combined with something the user has (a characteristic of that user, e.g., fingerprint) to gain access. Biometrics can also be one of the independent categories of credentials used for *multi-factor authentication (MFA)*. This is where defense is layered in hopes that even if a bad actor obtains two sets of credentials, there still will be at least one more barrier between the actor and their target.

Justin Orcutt
Security Awareness

What is it?
A state of understanding current security issues.

Why is it important?
Security awareness is important because employee mistakes are the number one cause of data breaches. Therefore, it is important to educate staff on security risks to help prevent cybersecurity incidents.

About Justin Orcutt
Justin Orcutt has worked with Fortune 500 companies to address information security and compliance concerns. Justin has supported incident response projects that investigated large-scale breaches. An active member of several organizations, including the Technology Association of Georgia, ISACA, and the Information Systems Security Association (ISSA), Justin is on the Gwinnett Tech Cybersecurity Program Advisory Board.

Email	jorcutt2017@gmail.com
Twitter	@jtech2014
LinkedIn	linkedin.com/in/justinorcutt

Why does a business professional need to know this?

Every business today needs to combat cybersecurity risks and, as such, must educate their employees and customers about the risks associated with their business.

Employees are primary targets for cybercriminals, and they need to understand how their actions can expose the business to a loss. Whether it is the risk of financial loss, loss of data, loss of privacy, or loss of confidential customer information, security awareness helps employees understand how to protect data.

Because employees are the first line of defense, they need to have a basic understanding of security risks. If employees have a baseline understanding of security issues, the business can be more agile combatting threats.

You can raise employee security awareness through effective training, but your efforts should not stop at training. Security awareness training is just one component of an overall security awareness program. Other components in such a program include newsletters, blogs, posters, teachable moments, computer-based training, security portals, and more.

Together, all of these elements can be the ingredients for a successful security awareness program. Although security specialists can create and deliver some aspects of a security awareness program, all business professionals are responsible for maintaining an awareness of potential vulnerabilities and the steps they can take to mitigate risk.

In addition to being a best practice, security awareness training is required to be in compliance with industry and governmental standards, including the *Payment Card Industry Data Security Standard (PCI DSS)*, which is a global standard, and the Health Insurance Portability and Accountability Act (HIPAA)[148] in the US.

Danyetta Fleming Magana
Situational Awareness

What is it?
An ongoing process to define an organization's risk and threat environment as it relates to its people, processes, policies, and technology.

Why is it important?
Situational awareness provides the foundation upon which to build a strategy for all other activities related to safeguarding your information and reducing cybersecurity risks. Every organization is unique in its mission, culture, and function; therefore, effective risk management requires that business professionals maintain situational awareness to ensure proper focus and perspective.

About Danyetta Fleming Magana
Danyetta Fleming Magana founded Covenant Security Solutions in 2003. Her goal is to change how we think about our information and find new and innovative ways to secure our digital assets. Danyetta is a Certified Information Systems Security Professional (CISSP), a globally recognized certification in the information security arena. In 2011, 2012, and 2014, her company was recognized by Diversity Business as one of the "Top 500 African-American Owned Businesses in the US." She is a graduate of the University of Illinois Urbana Champaign with a bachelor's degree in engineering.

Email	fleming_danyetta@covenantsec.com
Website	covenantsec.com
Twitter	@fleming_magana
LinkedIn	linkedin.com/in/covsec4u
Facebook	facebook.com/covenantcyber

Why does a business professional need to know this?

The success of any cybersecurity risk management program depends on the ability of an organization to protect information and digital assets. In order to define a cybersecurity risk strategy, business professionals and cybersecurity specialists must understand the environment their organization operates in. In other words, they must have good situational awareness of their environment.

The situational awareness process considers all aspects of an organization from supply chain to information technology in relation to potential cybersecurity vulnerabilities and threats. For example, what would be the impact on your organization if you lost critical privacy or intellectual property? Would such a loss require operations to cease for a period of time or even permanently? Can you manage the operational impact?

If you attempt to define a risk management program without good situational awareness, you are likely to waste resources on strategies and safeguards that either do not achieve an optimal Return on Investment (ROI) or are ineffective.

2013, the danger of losing situational awareness became clear to the department store chain Target when the company's vendor system was breached, costing the retailer millions of dollars and damaging its reputation[130][131]. Vendors often have access rights to intellectual property, privacy data, and information systems across multiple business units and functions. Understanding their role in your environment is key to developing an effective strategy to manage cybersecurity risks.

Holli Harrison
Behavioral Monitoring

What is it?
A form of anomaly detection that analyzes and correlates user activity on a computer or network to identify events and patterns that may require further investigation.

Why is it important?
Behavioral monitoring helps security teams quickly pinpoint unusual activity and act upon it. Also known as user and entity behavior analytics (UEBA), behavioral monitoring gathers data to build profiles for different types of users. It can then use those profiles to identify and flag potential threats. It has the potential to catch emerging threats before traditional, signature-based tools.

About Holli Harrison
Holli Harrison specializes in security controls, risk management and security education. She has helped government agencies, healthcare companies, universities, and technology companies improve their security postures through assessment, education, and consulting.

| Twitter | @security_person |
| LinkedIn | linkedin.com/in/holliharrison |

Why does a business professional need to know this?

Behavioral monitoring is an increasingly important tool for identifying and defending against cyberattacks that is becoming a larger part of security budgets. Gartner predicts that "60% of enterprise information security budgets will be allocated to rapid detection and response approaches by 2020, up from less than 10% in 2014"[11].

A behavioral monitoring system collects and uses data to build profiles for particular types of users based on role or location. Once profiles are built and activated, significant deviations from the profiles alert security analysts to the need for further review.

Here are some examples:

A remote employee usually accesses the *virtual private network (VPN)* from her home and from a nearby coffee shop. In the space of 30 minutes her login credentials are used from two different cities on different continents. Behavioral monitoring tools can detect the credentials being used from two places thousands of miles apart and raise an alert.

An accounts payable clerk usually works in the corporate office between 8 AM and 6 PM, Monday through Friday. As part of his usual work, he accesses the accounting system, a shared finance folder, the company intranet, and the inventory system. On his lunch break, he usually reads political news websites and occasionally listens to streaming news broadcasts during the day. Behavioral monitoring would flag these actions:

- Logging in from a different location
- Attempting to access different systems or files (source code, human resources files, or mergers and acquisitions information)
- Logging in at 1 AM
- Connecting to servers in China or Russia

Any of these activities taken alone could be legitimate user behavior that a security analyst could verify by talking to the user. Taken together, these events could indicate a security compromise. Behavioral analysis allows companies to move quickly to respond to threats and stop attackers before they can *exfiltrate* data or cause damage to the company's systems and data.

John Falkl
Non-repudiation

What is it?

The process of ensuring that an action was taken by a specific person or entity. In IT security, non-repudiation is the ability to validate that the contents of a message received can be verified as unchanged and also verified as having come from a specific person or entity.

Why is it important?

When dealing with electronic transactions, it's important to confirm with a high degree of certainty that actions or decisions were, in fact, taken by specific individuals or entities. Since hackers are getting better at impersonating identities, greater security measures must be implemented to ensure the integrity, accuracy, and authenticity of electronic transactions such as credit card purchases or digital signatures.

About John Falkl

John Falkl is the head of service excellence at Prolifics, a business solutions consulting organization. Prior to Prolifics, John was with IBM as the executive and IBM distinguished engineer responsible for service-oriented architecture (SOA) and application services governance, driving the convergence strategy for service governance and API management.

Email   jfalkl@aol.com
LinkedIn   linkedin.com/in/john-falkl-808aa03

Why does a business professional need to know this?

Business professionals need to be able to verify that actions, such as bank transfers, contracts, and credit card purchases, can be linked with a specific actor (person or entity). Non-repudiation methods help ensure the following:

- The action was not taken by a hacker impersonating someone.
- The actor cannot claim to have not taken the action.

In today's digital world, it is becoming increasingly important to verify that specific actions were taken by specific individuals. For transactions, such as financial transfers, that require greater integrity, organizations need to implement and enforce security measures that ensure the authenticity and intent of each transaction. For transactions, such as product surveys, where there is little or no business need to reliably identify a specific actor, it is less important to take such measures.

Measures to ensure non-repudiation include: notarization, *multi-factor authentication*, audit trails, *digital signatures*, and forensic analysis (e.g., handwriting analysis)[83].

There are multiple technologies available to implement and enforce non-repudiation. Measures to *authenticate* identity play an important part in ensuring that individuals are, in fact, who they assert themselves to be. *Digital certificates* and *encryption* can secure a message and ensure that its contents are not altered during transmission.

In an expanding digital economy, the integrity of your business depends on your ability to prove that each critical transaction was verifiably executed by a specific, identifiable person or process.

Emma Lilliestam
Privilege

What is it?
The range of actions an authenticated user or device is allowed to take in a system.

Why is it important?
A good society works like this: we expect promises to be kept, contracts to be honored, and a lost wallet to be returned. However, when applied to your IT infrastructure, such a mindset leaves your system wide open to an insider or an unhappy former employee. Privilege management gives you detailed control over the permissions given to each user and device.

About Emma Lilliestam
Emma Lilliestam is a Swedish IT security architect. She has previously worked in support as well as in information security and is now the head of Devops at a Swedish IoT startup, Ewa Home.

Email	emma.lilliestam@gmail.com
Website	ewahome.com
Twitter	@emalstm
LinkedIn	se.linkedin.com/in/emma-lilliestam-0122a789

Why does a business professional need to know this?

Giving your house key to a neighbor so they can water your plants does not mean you want to allow them to look through your closets or bedroom drawers. However, most of us do not have the technical means to restrict access in this way; we either give access to the entire house, or we don't give access at all. Giving your key to a neighbor relies on implicit trust. You trust that your neighbor will not try on your underwear or eat all your cookies.

To put it mildly, this is not an ideal trust model for your IT infrastructure; you need a model that relies on least privilege, which gives each user only the privileges needed to perform their job duties and nothing more.

In many organizations, the highest possible access rights are given to system administrators. Companies that blindly trust system administrators open themselves to unnecessary risk. It is safer to have fine-grained control over privileges and give each administrator only the privileges needed to carry out their assigned tasks. For example, an administrator responsible for the payroll database probably doesn't need access to the customer database.

To do this you need to implement an access-level classification scheme and have procedures that support your daily operations. This approach eliminates the need to give users higher levels of access than they need. This would be the equivalent of putting a password on your underwear drawer, making it inaccessible to your neighbor who has only the front door key.

Sarah Granger
Firewall

What is it?

A network security system built into hardware or software that monitors network traffic and controls incoming and outgoing traffic based on a set of rules.

Why is it important?

Firewalls enable system administrators to monitor and control network traffic coming into and out of their systems. Firewalls provide a first line of defense against network-based cybersecurity attacks. They are also used to censor information by blocking traffic to and from certain sites.

About Sarah Granger

Sarah Granger is a former network security engineer and author of *The Digital Mystique: How the Culture of Connectivity Can Empower Your Life – Online and Off*. She previously contributed to two books on cybersecurity: *Diplomacy, Development and Security in the Information Age* and *Ethical Hacking*.

Email	sarah@sarahgranger.com
Website	sarahgranger.com
Twitter	@sarahgranger
LinkedIn	linkedin.com/in/sarahgranger
Facebook	facebook.com/sarahgranger.author

Why does a business professional need to know this?

Firewalls first came into use as packet filters that analyzed data in packets and identified which data was safe to continue moving forward and which data needed to be removed or stopped. Up to that point, network administrators had to choose between keeping networks connected to the internet, allowing most data to come and go, or disconnecting networks completely, leaving them physically isolated.

Modern firewalls work in hardware and software through an established set of rules to determine what comes in and what goes out. Firewalls are considered a first line of defense against unwanted intruders, information, or code. They can be used to keep out hackers or merely to cut down on *spam*.

Two common types of firewalls are network firewalls, which monitor and filter communications between networks (e.g., between an internal corporate network and the external internet), and host-based firewalls, which monitor and filter communications coming in and out of an individual computer. A firewall can block a communication packet based on the port it attempts to pass through or the type of content it contains.

The most famous firewall is the Great Firewall of China[48], which the Chinese government uses to block people inside China from accessing sites and services containing information prohibited by the government. Google, for example, is blocked in China, so Chinese internet users generally must use the Chinese internet search engine Baidu, which operates through censorship filters. The Chinese firewall has been surprisingly successful at blocking vast amounts of information.

John Armstrong
Encryption

What is it?
The process of encoding a message or information in such a way that only authorized parties can read it.

Why is it important?
Encryption is important to our personal, business, community, and national security. Criminals, competitors, or hostile governments may seek to exploit weak or non-existent encryption to hack systems or steal data. Strong, well-managed encryption renders content unreadable to anyone who does not have authorized access.

About John Armstrong
John Armstrong is chief marketing officer (CMO) at Zettaset, a leader in big data security. A former independent consultant, John previously served as vice president and chief analyst at Gartner. He has held key marketing positions at Yipes (Reliant), Madge Networks (Avaya), and Bay Networks (Nortel). John received an MA from the Annenberg School, University of Southern California.

Email	armstrong@calcentral.com
Twitter	@exit17
LinkedIn	linkedin.com/in/armstrong

Why does a business professional need to know this?

In our interconnected world of computers and networks, strong encryption helps prevent unauthorized parties from accessing sensitive data. Encryption protects an individual's personal financial details and passwords when banking online and prevents cell phone conversations from being overheard by eavesdroppers.

More broadly, encryption protects critical civil and government infrastructure, including communication networks, power grids, transportation infrastructure, and defense systems. Securing data and systems requires more than just encryption, but encryption is a critical component of information security. While it is mostly invisible, encryption is used every day by anyone who uses a phone, the internet, or a bank card.

The cost of neglecting data security is high. The *2017 Ponemon Cost of Data Breach Study*[45] showed that the average data breach cost a company $3.62 million, a small decrease from 2016, but the overall trend has been upward. 2016 saw a 29% increase from 2013 and a 5% increase since 2015.

In addition, they found that the average cost of a breach per customer record is $141, which even for a company with only a few thousand customer records could be devastating.

Keirsten Brager
Sandboxing

What is it?

The practice of isolating *malware*, or software that is suspected to contain malware, within a contained or quarantined environment to observe and study its communications, infection vectors, and other behavioral heuristics.

Why is it important?

Sandboxing allows security researchers to investigate malware execution, heuristics, and communications within an isolated environment and aids in the development of *indicators of compromise (IOC)* and *anti-malware signatures*.

About Keirsten Brager

Keirsten Brager, Certified Information Systems Security Professional (CISSP) and CompTIA Advanced Security Practitioner (CASP), is the founder of hiddencyberfigures.com. This project is dedicated to increasing the number of minority women in cybersecurity by mentoring and sharing success stories of overlooked talent. Keirsten is a security engineer by trade, graduate student, CompTIA exam developer, and public speaker.

Email	kwbrager@gmail.com
Website	hiddencyberfigures.com
Twitter	@HiddenCybFigures
LinkedIn	linkedin.com/in/kbrager

Why does a business professional need to know this?

Sandboxing is one of many techniques security researchers use to observe complex malware, including *advanced persistent threats (APTs)*. This technique contains malware within a virtual environment that allows it to function only within predefined and enforced limits.

By using virtual environments to mimic vulnerable targets, a cybersecurity specialist can execute malware under controlled conditions. Malware can be unpredictable and difficult to contain in the wild, and isolating it can be the only way to determine the mechanism by which it infects, proliferates, and communicates.

Of particular importance to cybersecurity specialists are the *IOCs* that can be garnered from sandboxing. Attackers often leverage techniques that exhibit distinct exploit patterns. These patterns can be observed using sandboxing techniques, then used to identify similarly functioning malware and, potentially, attribute the malware to a particular source.

Although sandboxing is a viable tool for researching malware behavior, sophisticated APTs can detect the existence of a virtual environment (i.e. sandbox) and either not execute or disable themselves, making it difficult or impossible for a researcher to investigate[115]. However, sandboxing remains an important technique in a cybersecurity specialist's arsenal[114].

Linda Maepa
Hardening

What is it?
The act or process of making a network, data repository, sensor, computer system, software, or other equipment resistant to unauthorized access or damage.

Why is it important?
Unauthorized access is one of the primary catalysts for operational, financial, strategic, legal, and other damage to an organization. These breaches also increase the risk of harm to third parties, including customers, patients, and other stakeholders. Hardening hardware, software, and data systems is a key risk mitigation strategy.

About Linda Maepa
Linda Maepa brings several decades of information systems, cybersecurity, and systems science experience to the energy sector. She currently leads an energy and transportation advisory and project development firm. She is an active advisor to academia, government, and industry worldwide regarding energy and economic security, energy sector cyber-physical security, risk management, energy storage, and project finance. She holds a BS degree from the California Institute of Technology (Caltech) and is currently writing the first book in the *Cyber-physical Security and Battery System Design series*.

Email	linda@electroferocious.com
Website	electroferocious.com
LinkedIn	linkedin.com/in/lmaepa

Why does a business professional need to know this?

Hardening is necessary when there is a mission-critical need to:

- Protect information, content, or application data such as health records, credit card information, intellectual property, or location information
- Ensure continuous availability and reliable performance of facilities such as electric grids, factories, or data centers
- Safeguard hardware and other resources, such as computer servers, passenger vehicles, building sensor networks, or point-of-sale systems

Hardening is an ongoing, never-ending process that business professionals must understand and support. Frequently, the value of hardening – and the need to invest in workforce development and processes – is not apparent until a high-profile failure occurs.

A recent galvanizing event was the loss of credit card information for 40 million Target customers during the 2013 Christmas season[53]. This breach resulted in a 46% drop in profits for that quarter, a CEO exit, and nearly $150 million in settlements. The vulnerabilities exposed included significant failures in hardening networking and other equipment found in most businesses.

In 2016, a *Distributed Denial-of-Service (DDoS)* attack left Twitter and Reddit inaccessible for many US web users[54]. Similar questions about the amount of hardening applied to in-flight entertainment systems were raised in 2015, when a cybersecurity researcher was accused of unauthorized access to flight systems and issuing a command to one of the airplane engines that resulted in a change of flight movement[55].

Security industry analysis indicates that crisis planning and the application of lessons learned from a breach can minimize losses. Effective teams should be multi-disciplinary to ensure deep subject-matter expertise and capabilities. Funding for these teams should be available from product/service conception to end of life, because hardening approaches can differ at each point in the lifecycle.

Security culture has developed a number of ways to share lessons learned and build practical expertise in identifying and fixing vulnerabilities across a wide array of equipment and software. Investing in continued learning, such as conferences and certification, empowers cybersecurity teams to plan for, prepare for, and address the ever-shifting threat landscape.

Planning, Management, and Controls

> Organizations need help to address the question of whether the organization's investment in information security management is effective, fit for purpose to react, defend, and respond to the continually changing cyber-risk environment.
> —Edward Humphreys, Convener ISO/IEC 27004 working group

Managing cybersecurity is not separate or distinct from managing other aspects of your organization. Well-managed cybersecurity is as much a strategic advantage as any other well-managed business resource. Cybersecurity risk is business risk.

There is no such thing as total protection from security risks. Nevertheless, you must identify risks, assess them, and implement plans to minimize them. A successful plan must include a tracking mechanism and contingency strategies for mitigating risks. You need to weigh the cost of cybersecurity measures against the benefits and decide what is optimal for your organization.

Fortunately, you don't have to reinvent the wheel. Here are some frameworks that outline ways to assess and manage cybersecurity:

- **ISO/IEC 27000:** this family of standards – known as Information Security Management Systems (ISMS) and ISO27k – defines best practices for an information security management system. Systems that meet the criteria can be certified as compliant with the standard[138].
- **NIST 800:** describes United States federal government computer security policies, procedures, and guidelines, which are also useful to businesses and other organizations[3].

- **Center for Internet Security:** defines basic, foundational, and organizational actions to protect your organization and data from known cyberattack vectors[8].

These frameworks include components for assessment, planning, measurement, tracking, and reporting. Any of these standards families can help your organization manage the security of its assets.

Security planning starts with a *vulnerability assessment* to identify what might cause a security disruption. The output of the assessment is a set of issues, which are noted in a *risk register*. You address how you will respond to potential disruptions in an *incident response plan* and plan for the aftermath of a disruption in a *business continuity plan*. The *business impact assessment* requires further analysis of the interdependencies and defines priorities. Templates for each of these plans are included in NIST Special Publication 800-34[23].

The Planning Process

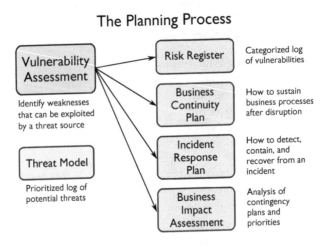

The output of the vulnerability assessment can also be used for *threat modeling*. A threat model considers *attack vectors*, ranks them, and documents how to mitigate them. The threat model helps you determine how to best use the resources you have available for security.

Terms in this section:

- Governance, Risk Management, Compliance (GRC)
- Application Risk Governance
- Vulnerability Assessment
- Business Impact Assessment (BIA)
- Business Continuity Plan
- Incident Response Plan
- Chief Information Security Officer (CISO)
- Risk Register
- Kill Chain
- Metrics
- Audit
- Threat Modeling
- Static Application Security Testing (SAST)
- Penetration Testing

Flavio Valenzuela
Governance, Risk Management, Compliance (GRC)

What is it?

A combination of three approaches that organizations use to demonstrate compliance with international standards, global rules, laws, and state regulations. Referred to as IT GRC when a company uses information technology (IT) to apply GRC.

Why is it important?

Governance, risk management, compliance (GRC) is often implemented by companies that are growing globally to maintain consistent policies, processes, and procedures across all parts of the organization. It is important for business professionals to understand and follow the internal information security rules, company risk factors, and industry requirements that drive the implementation of GRC in order to ensure that the company as a whole remains compliant.

About Flavio Valenzuela

Flavio Valenzuela has broad experience in finance, telecommunications, information security, and international markets in Latin America and the Caribbean. He has bachelor's degrees in letters/science from De La Salle (HS) and in business administration from Pontificia Universidad Católica Madre y Maestra (PUCMM) and a master's degree in economics from PUCMM. His certifications include Payment Card Industry Professional (PCIP) and Certified Information System Security Professional (CISSP).

Email	flaviovalenzuela@gmail.com
Website	darasecurity.com
LinkedIn	linkedin.com/in/flavio-valenzuela-64261843
Facebook	facebook.com/flavio.valenzuela.7

Why does a business professional need to know this?

For companies to provide quality products or services, grow, and achieve success, they need an efficient vision, correct guidelines, internal controls, and mature operations.

Compliance is central to this effort, because companies must adhere to international standards, requirements, and certifications to succeed. Compliance is a combination of internal processes that ensure that all operational procedures follow guidelines and specifications from industry regulations, local laws, and information security best practices.

Business professionals should consider incorporating innovative solutions and technologies designed to protect intellectual property (content) and personally-identifiable or sensitive personal information (data) from the prying eyes of competitors, disgruntled employees, and mischievous pranksters. However, introducing new technologies introduces risk. Digitally-savvy organizations adopt *risk management* best practices to reduce potential negative impacts from these cybersecurity efforts.

Risk management is the discovery, evaluation, and prioritization of business risks. Risk management activities involve determining, minimizing, and controlling the probability or impact of unfortunate events. Risk managers work to help organizations develop rules, adopt controls, and take steps designed to both protect information assets and eliminate cybersecurity vulnerabilities. Risk managers also develop response plans and proactive protection strategies focused on limiting the impact of cyberattacks.

Risk management and compliance efforts must be aligned to address these needs, which leads companies to adopt *governance*. Governance refers to a set of policies, processes, and procedures that define how a company ensures that critical systems and sensitive information are kept secure, confidential, and available.

Graeme Fleck
Application Risk Governance

What is it?
Controls to ensure that software applications are developed and operated in accordance with an organization's requirements and risk tolerance levels[2].

Why is it important?
Application risk governance provides a framework to ensure an appropriate balance between security and operations.

About Graeme Fleck
Graeme Fleck has been part of the Hewlett Packard Enterprise Software team for four years, working in focused roles across application development, IT security, and IT operations management. As part of the marketing and sales organization, he has worked closely with HPE Fortify, presenting and understanding the security challenges facing global businesses.

Email   fleck@hpe.com
Twitter   @fleck_hp
LinkedIn   linkedin.com/in/tech-fleck
Facebook   facebook.com/graeme.fleck.7

Why does a business professional need to know this?

Everywhere, disruptive technologies and applications are introducing risk to organizations both internally and on the web. Application risk governance provides a framework to identify and remove quality issues that pose an unacceptable level of risk at all stages of software delivery, from planning to production.

Successful governance can be achieved only if the entire process is efficiently mapped, measured, and monitored. Policies and procedures must be well-documented, and employees must have incentives to follow them.

The Open Web App Security Project (OWASP) identifies processes that result in improved governance[4]. These processes include the following:

- Software security integration into the software development lifecycle
- Security requirements identification
- Design security review
- Architecture security review
- Security code review
- Security testing
- Deployment security review
- Release security review

These processes follow the premise that governance can be achieved more effectively by design than by re-examination.

The US Department of Homeland Security advocates best practice in software development and a "Build Security In" approach as part of a comprehensive software assurance professional competency model[7].

It is important to remember: not all quality issues are security issues, but all security issues are quality issues.

Jeff Schaffzin
Vulnerability Assessment

What is it?
A process for defining, identifying, classifying, and prioritizing potential weaknesses in an organization's computer, network, and communications infrastructure, also known as vulnerability analysis or security assessment.

Why is it important?
When conducted correctly, results from a vulnerability assessment can be used to define or update an organization's internal and external network as well as its information security policies.

About Jeff Schaffzin
Jeff Schaffzin is a corporate, product, strategy, marketing, and business development expert with over 20 years of experience in high tech, covering industries such as security (network, cyber, physical), enterprise software, business intelligence and analytics, big data, the internet of things (IoT), cloud technologies (software as a service (SaaS) and platform as a service (PaaS)), mobile, marketing technology, and financial technology.

Jeff is currently the managing director and principal with Genysys Group (Silicon Valley) and heads product marketing and management for SecureALL Corporation.

Email	jschaffzin@genysysgroup.com
Twitter	@JeffSchaffzin
LinkedIn	linkedin.com/in/jeffschaffzin

Why does a business professional need to know this?

Vulnerability assessments provide cybersecurity specialists, and the organizations they serve, with a reasonable level of assurance that their information is safeguarded against known threats such as *viruses, adware, spyware, trojans, worms, backdoors, bots*, and *Potentially Unwanted Programs (PUP)*[147].

Vulnerability assessments help cybersecurity specialists determine where to allocate finite resources to minimize the potential for security breaches. They also help organizations determine what course of action to follow if – and when – threats are discovered. Business professionals must understand the elements of a vulnerability assessment and support their cybersecurity specialists in creating one and keeping it up to date.

For organizations that are mandated to follow specialized security standards (e.g., HIPAA[148], PCI DSS[149], or GDPR[150]) vulnerability assessments can help identify areas of weakness that need *hardening*.

Vulnerability assessments may include the following:

- **Cybersecurity audits:** *audits* to evaluate and demonstrate compliance with government-imposed regulations. Cybersecurity audits have both a tactical and strategic component – tactically, they help organizations comply with security standards, and strategically, they help organizations monitor their internal security efforts.
- **Penetration tests:** authorized testing of a computer system or network with the intention of finding vulnerabilities. *Penetration tests* are typically intended to counter specific threats, such as attempts to steal customer data, gain administrative privileges, or modify salary information.
- **White/grey/black-box assessments:** three different approaches to vulnerability assessments. The color refers to how much internal information is given to the tester: white box gives the tester access to all internal information, black box gives the tester zero internal information, and grey box gives the tester a limited amount of information, for example the internal data structures.

William McBorrough
Business Impact Assessment (BIA)

What is it?

A systematic process by which an organization gathers information about its essential business functions and processes and evaluates the potential impact to the organization if those functions and processes were interrupted or otherwise adversely affected. Also referred to as a business impact analysis.

Why is it important?

This term is important because it helps organizations prioritize the allocation of time and resources to prevent, manage, and recover from incidents that affect critical business operations and assets. A business impact assessment also provides information to help create an *incident response plan* and a *business continuity plan*.

About William McBorrough

William J. McBorrough is the co-founder of and CEO at MCGlobalTech, a Washington DC-based information security management consulting firm. For more than 19 years, Mr. McBorrough has demonstrated success as an administrator, engineer, architect, consultant, manager, and practice leader, developing cost-effective solutions to support the strategic and operational goals of client organizations in the areas of enterprise information security risk management, IT governance, security organization development and management, and government information assurance and compliance.

Email	wjm4@mcglobaltech.com
Website	mcglobaltech.com
Twitter	@infosec3t
LinkedIn	linkedin.com/in/mcborrough
Facebook	facebook.com/MCGlobalTech

Why does a business professional need to know this?

Conducting a business impact assessment (BIA) can help you see how security and risk management relates to the critical functions and overall mission of your organization. Security must support those functions and that mission.

Implementing security controls and managing cybersecurity risks costs time, money, and resources. A business impact assessment helps business professionals balance priorities and apply resources where they can have the greatest effect.

A business impact assessment is critical to both the risk management program and the *business continuity plan,* which enable an organization to assess and manage risks to critical assets and functions and recover and continue business operations when those assets and functions are negatively affected.

Essential questions that must be answered as part of the BIA include the following:

- What information systems and functions are critical to the mission of the organization?
- What do those systems and functions depend on?
- If those systems and functions are impaired or interrupted, how quickly must they resume before the organization incurs a significant loss or unacceptable business impact?

Business professionals must work with cybersecurity professionals to help identify security risks to the organization's business operations and information systems. A business impact assessment can help prioritize efforts to mitigate the potential impact of those risks to the organization.

Dale Shulmistra
Business Continuity Plan

What is it?
A plan that allows an organization to remain operational at acceptable, predefined levels of operation despite disruptions resulting from human, technical, or natural causes.

Why is it important?
With more and more companies becoming heavily reliant on data to drive decisions, any loss of that data – even short-term – can bring business to a halt and have dire effects on the bottom line.

About Dale Shulmistra
Dale Shulmistra has over 15 years of expertise in information technology, specializing in business continuity. He is the co-founder of Invenio IT. Dale is responsible for shaping the company's technology initiatives and selecting, designing, implementing, and supporting business continuity solutions and services to bolster client operational efficiencies and eliminate downtime.

Email dale@invenioIT.com
Website invenioIT.com
Twitter @invenioIT
LinkedIn linkedin.com/in/daleshulmistra
Facebook facebook.com/InvenioIT

Why does a business professional need to know this?

While cybersecurity plays an important role in keeping a business safe and operational, it is only part of the solution. Attacks now use advanced technology, big data, artificial intelligence, and analytics in ways that rival some of the most innovative and sophisticated methods being used by legitimate businesses around the world. New strains of malware that exploit *zero-day* vulnerabilities are being developed every day, making it impossible for security policies, solutions, and training to keep pace, let alone stay ahead of determined cybercriminals.

As a result, the only way to protect an organization is to have a business continuity plan and supporting technology to ensure that company servers and data are always backed up and recoverable, even in the face of the most aggressive attack.

In contrast with an *incident response plan*, which outlines the immediate response to a breach, a business continuity plan focuses on the steps needed to keep a business going after an attack. An effective business continuity plan must create a response team to coordinate pre-event planning, testing, communications, and backups as well as post-event tasks such as maintaining access to business records and ensuring continuous IT operations[22].

Cybersecurity measures can prevent many threats, but with the level of sophistication and *social engineering* techniques used by cybercriminals today, eventually one will get through. That is why business professionals must work with cybersecurity specialists to build a strong business continuity plan.

M.K. Palmore
Incident Response Plan

What is it?

A comprehensive, step-by-step series of actions to be followed by an organization's computer security incident response team (CSIRT) and business operations personnel following a verified cybersecurity incident to reduce the overall impact of the incident.

Why is it important?

When properly implemented, an incident response plan can help ensure an effective response to security incidents and help mitigate the effects of a potentially serious event. The presence of a well-rehearsed plan has proven to reduce the financial impact of security incidents.

About M.K. Palmore

M.K. Palmore serves as the leader of the FBI San Francisco cyber branch. His responsibilities include the operational management of several teams of cyber intrusion investigators, computer scientists, and digital forensics personnel. Mr. Palmore joined the FBI in 1997. His certifications include Certified Information Systems Security Professional (CISSP) and Certified Information Security Manager (CISM). He earned a BS from the US Naval Academy and an MBA from Pepperdine University. Prior to the FBI, Mr. Palmore served as a commissioned officer in the US Marine Corps.

Email	malcolm.palmore@gmail.com
Website	security-leadership.com
Twitter	@mk_palmore
LinkedIn	linkedin.com/in/m-k-palmore-cism-cissp-a0a71614

Why does a business professional need to know this?

An incident response plan serves as a cornerstone to effective mitigation and remediation following a breach or other information security (InfoSec) incident. Full implementation, practice, and awareness of the plan helps reduce response and recovery times following an incident. The plan provides for pre-breach practice or table-top sessions and outlines the roles and responsibilities of incident handlers and business operations personnel in responding to a security incident.

An incident response plan serves as a major component of the preparation, identification, containment, eradication, recovery, and lessons-learned cycle of incident handling procedures. It can also serve as a vital component of business continuity and disaster response planning. And because the plan is a living document, it can be updated to ensure proper response and alignment with the changing needs of the business.

The incident response plan complements the *business continuity plan*. The business continuity plan focuses on keeping the business running, while the incident response plan focuses on the attack itself and the company's response. Both are critical to building a resilient organization.

In addition to InfoSec units, others within non-technical business units have responsibilities following an incident. These departments include business operations, human resources, legal, communications/PR, and finance. Responsibility for developing the incident response plan falls under the Chief Information Security Officer (CISO) or a duly nominated representative, most likely the leader of the CSIRT.

Failure to develop and implement a plan has historically resulted in high-profile security failures in both the private and public sectors. An inadequate response to a high-profile breach or incident usually indicates that there was a poorly executed or ill-conceived incident response plan.

Todd Fitzgerald
CISO

What is it?
Chief Information Security Officer. The most senior individual responsible for protecting an organization's information assets.

Why is it important?
The CISO has overall responsibility for the information security program for an organization. The CISO works closely with executive management and business stakeholders to protect information assets.

About Todd Fitzgerald
Todd Fitzgerald is managing director/CISO, CISO Spotlight. He was named 2016-17 Chicago CISO of the Year and ranked Top 50 Information Security Executive. He has authored 3 books: *Information Security Governance Simplified: From the Boardroom to the Keyboard*, *CISO Leadership: Essential Principles for Success (ISC2)*, and *E-C Council Certified Chief Information Security Officer Body of Knowledge*, and he has contributed to a dozen others. Todd has held senior leadership positions at Northern Trust, Grant Thornton International, ManpowerGroup, WellPoint, Zeneca/Syngenta, IMS Health, and American Airlines.

Email	tfitzgerald@cisospotlight.com
Twitter	@securityfitz
LinkedIn	linkedin.com/in/toddfitzgerald

Why does a business professional need to know this?

The CISO is charged with providing an efficient and effective security program, which includes retaining skilled cybersecurity specialists and documenting and automating cybersecurity processes and procedures. Business professionals should know and work with the CISO and his or her team to build a secure environment.

The CISO works with management stakeholders to allocate an appropriate budget for cybersecurity; acquire the necessary personnel, tools, and resources; and create and execute plans for improving cybersecurity maturity. The CISO is accountable for identifying and communicating relevant information security threats, balancing the competing needs of business operations and information security, and leading the cybersecurity team as it works towards these objective. Cybersecurity maturity occurs over time as more investments are made, processes are refined, and tools are integrated into a long-term plan.

The CISO is responsible for ensuring that appropriate policies, standards, procedures, and guidelines exist within the organization to reduce overall risk and comply with regulatory and privacy requirements. Administrative, technical, and operational controls collectively fulfill this objective.

For example, a cybersecurity analyst may be assigned to implement controls that aggregate and correlate security events to detect malicious behavior against critical information assets. The CISO is responsible for warning stakeholders about the risk of potential malicious events, putting monitoring procedures in place, ensuring that oversight and secondary quality controls are present, and creating a monitoring strategy that reflects the organizations tolerance for risk.

Simon Puleo
Kill Chain

What is it?
The attack lifecycle or sequence of phases that malicious hackers use to exploit their targets.

Why is it important?
Cybersecurity professionals can create winning security and readiness programs by understanding the methods of their adversaries.

About Simon Puleo
Simon Puleo, Certified Ethical Hacker (CEH), is an educator/trainer by day and a security researcher at night. As a global enablement manager at Micro Focus, he helps employees and customers implement identity-powered security with an emphasis on access control, including multi-factor authentication and identity governance. Previously, he worked for Hewlett Packard Enterprise Security, focusing on application security, encryption key management, and security information and event management (SIEM). Simon is a thought leader actively engaged in researching the cyber-threat landscape and sharing his perspectives in seminars and articles.

Email	Simon.Puleo@gmail.com
Twitter	@simon_puleo
LinkedIn	linkedin.com/in/simonpuleo

Why does a business professional need to know this?

Understanding the kill chain helps cybersecurity professionals detect an attacker's perspective and helps business professionals understand the process that cybersecurity specialists use when investigating a breach.

Understanding each phase of the kill chain and how those phases relate to the IT landscape of your organization can help you develop the policies, controls, and preparations needed to defend against attacks.

The kill chain phases include the following:

1. **Reconnaissance:** attackers discover information about their target using a combination of profiles and vulnerabilities.
2. **Infiltration:** attackers weaponize the information to break into vulnerable systems, typically through network vulnerabilities or social engineering.
3. **Exploitation:** after breaking in, attackers exploit their access and hunt for valuable targets, including email archives, credit card data, and customer records.
4. **Exfiltration:** *exfiltration* is the process attackers use to capture and remove data. This can be done all at once or over a period of time.
5. **Monetization or media release:** criminals motivated by money typically sell data on the *dark web* to the highest bidder; those motivated for political reasons are more likely to deliver data directly to the media or WikiLeaks.

A good defensive practice is to map the kill chain to high-risk targets (for example an email archive), evaluate out how an attacker would go about stealing the archive, and then put controls and policies in place to block a cybercriminal at each phase, effectively breaking the kill chain[71].

Keyaan Williams
Metrics

What is it?
A quantifiable measurement used to help organizations evaluate performance.

Why is it important?
Metrics provide a standard for measuring the performance of governance programs and controls established to protect an organization's assets, interests, and resources.

About Keyaan Williams
Keyaan Williams represents a mosaic of experiences including cybersecurity leadership, military service, higher education, and board governance. Keyaan is a risk management and governance consultant who helps global security leaders transform their programs by running them like a business. He also serves on the international board of directors for the Information System Security Association (ISSA), an organization dedicated to advancing individual growth, managing technology risk, and protecting critical information and infrastructure.

Email	keyaan.williams@phaze5.net
Twitter	@KeyaanWilliams
LinkedIn	linkedin.com/in/keyaan

Why does a business professional need to know this?

Metrics help business professionals evaluate the level of performance achieved by their cybersecurity initiatives. Good metrics depend on good data and a consistent model for interpreting that data.

The foundation of good data is context, which determines the significance of a metric. For example, metrics about perimeter defenses have a different context than metrics about compliance with policies and procedures. Once the context is understood, cybersecurity specialists can identify meaningful things to measure.

Metrics can apply to anything; however, cybersecurity metrics should focus on information critical for protecting an organization: asset information, impact information, threat information, and controls information.

The effectiveness of cybersecurity metrics also depends on the model used to analyze the data. Many business disciplines use predictive models to forecast an expected outcome based on available data. Within cybersecurity, frequency distributions provide an effective model for metrics because they support observations about the effectiveness of different initiatives over time. This approach helps establish an initial benchmark that the organization can use as a reference to highlight the extent to which an initiative is successful or failing.

Example: An organization establishes a baseline with the average occurrence (mean frequency) of a successful attack = [x]. Based on risk tolerance, the stability, increase, or decrease of [x] allows the organization to measure the effectiveness of existing controls and decide what additional steps are appropriate to reduce the frequency of successful attacks.

Metrics, in and of themselves, do not prevent breaches. However, good metrics provide information to justify investment in the tools, products, and personnel needed to improve security programs. Without metrics, it is difficult for management to know where to focus resources to achieve meaningful outcomes

Terrie Diaz
Audit

What is it?
A systematic investigation of network and system activities and events.

Why is it important?
Auditing evaluates the who, what, where, and when of events on a network, which helps managers identify critical events that may have an impact on their organization.

About Terrie Diaz

Terrie Diaz is Cisco's government certification team technical lead and is responsible for Cisco's Common Criteria evaluations. She is well-versed in US and international certification requirements and is an active member in many of the global technical communities responsible for writing the collaborative protection profiles in which Common Criteria evaluations are performed.

Terrie is a Certified Information Systems Security Professional (CISSP) with over 30 years of experience in IT and system security, supply chain risk management, and program management. She has a bachelor of science degree in business management and retired from the US military after serving for 21 years.

Email   tediaz@cisco.com
LinkedIn   linkedin.com/in/terriediazmsg

Why does a business professional need to know this?

Business professionals need information about events that are essential to ensure continuous business operation, security of sensitive data, and availability of resources.

Knowing what and how much to audit is an important decision. Auditing every event provides too much information and is resource intensive. Auditing no events leaves system administrators unaware of hacking attempts, the health of devices on the network, configuration changes, and other events, such as password changes.

Just as important as auditing specific events is reviewing event records. If no one is paying attention to the data being collected, then auditing serves no purpose. Auditing provides a wealth of information in real time, and reviewing event logs provides important information to ensure that proper action can be taken.

System administrators configure systems to ensure that audit records are generated for the required auditable events. Here are some examples of auditable events:

- Failed login attempts
- Network connection attempts
- An administrator opening or shutting down a network port

Auditing software typically generates a record for each event that records the date and time of the event, the type of event, and the person who initiated the event. Audit records can be difficult to read in their raw form, but system administrators typically use programs that search for patterns and generate reports to summarize results.

Audits can reveal vulnerabilities before they are exploited by attackers. For example, an audit of IT practices in the town of Geneseo, New York, revealed lax procedures and deficiencies that left the town's computer systems vulnerable to attack[9]. This is just one example of many instances where audits revealed serious deficiencies in cybersecurity.

John Diamant
Threat Modeling

What is it?

A formal method to identify, characterize, and prioritize risks and threats, typically with the goal of reducing them, also known as *threat analysis* or *risk analysis*.

Why is it important?

Most software is riddled with vulnerabilities, and software is pervasive in devices such as phones, cars, voting machines, etc. Threat modeling is one of the most effective ways to avoid and find vulnerabilities.

About John Diamant

John Diamant, Certified Information Systems Security Professional (CISSP), Certified Secure Software Lifecycle Professional (CSSLP), founded one of the world's largest technology company's secure development programs where he is a Distinguished Technologist (top 1/2% of technologists). He is an inventor on 11 issued patents, and is both software assurance chief technologist and applications security strategist. He has published articles in IEEE Security & Privacy, presented at conferences such as RSA, and his interviews have been seen by over 1/2 million people and reported by mainstream media including CNN, The Wall Street Journal, and many more. He has briefed senior staff of a joint Congressional subcommittee.

Email	john.diamant@gmail.com
Website	dxc.technology/applications_security
LinkedIn	linkedin.com/in/johndiamant

Why does a business professional need to know this?

Threat modeling assesses, architects, and designs security into software, avoiding many vulnerabilities and reducing the severity of others. Techniques used in threat modeling, such as *attack surface* analysis and reducing unnecessary elevation of *privilege*, can avoid thousands of vulnerabilities at once, without having to find and fix them individually.

Business professionals should know about threat modeling because it is the single secure software design practice used by all SAFECode members. The Software Assurance Forum (SAFECode) is a non-profit organization exclusively dedicated to increasing trust in information and communications technology products and services through advancement of effective software assurance methods[144].

Developers who do not use threat analysis often fail to create secure-by-design software, leading to poor security quality. Architectural threat analysis and modeling significantly increase robustness and resilience, dramatically reducing the number and severity of vulnerabilities[145].

A threat analysis of Linux software avoided more than 100 vulnerabilities, which required security patches or updates to be developed, tested, released, and installed, all at a significant cost to the developer and software users[145]. Despite the cost, this was the best-case scenario. The worst case would have been a serious data breach, such as the Equifax breach, which exposed Social Security numbers and other sensitive information for more than half of the U.S. adult population, rendering Social Security numbers obsolete as a security measure, costing the CEO his job, and enabling countless identity thefts.

Threat analysis and modeling should be preceded by a security requirements gap analysis to identify missing or incompletely addressed security requirements and controls. This ensures that those conducting the threat analysis understand the security requirements and controls required to enable appropriate security properties[146].

We need to apply the lessons from past decades that tell us that quality (and thus security) must be designed in, and we can't expect to simply test it out. Although software developers sometimes do threat modeling without specific, or only brief, training, this practice is analogous to do-it-yourself surgery. To avoid a false sense of security, have independent experts perform risk analysis and threat modeling.

Lucas von Stockhausen
Static Application Security Testing

What is it?
A test for security vulnerabilities that looks at the source code or binary of an application without running it.

Why is it important?
Static Application Security Testing (SAST) can be used before an application is executable, enabling early and regular tests for security vulnerabilities. SAST allows developers to fix problems during the development phase of an application and at a much lower cost than when the code is in quality assurance (QA) or production.

About Lucas von Stockhausen
Lucas von Stockhausen has 10 years' experience in application security with a deep knowledge of static, dynamic, and interactive application security testing as well as remote access security program technologies.

As senior product manager and application security strategist, he has a deep understanding of how companies implement these solutions, including processes such as the building security in maturity model (BSIMM) and the software assurance maturity model (OpenSAMM).

Email   lvonstockhausen@microfocus.com
Website   fortify.com

Why does a business professional need to know this?

Business professionals and developers need to understand the basics of SAST and its essential role in catching vulnerabilities early in the development process. This is especially critical for environments where there is limited time for final product testing.

SAST analyzes an application for security vulnerabilities without executing the code. SAST looks for insecure coding patterns in the source code, bytecode, or binary of the application. SAST can help identify the exact lines of code where an attack might occur. SAST can then recommend how to fix the vulnerability.

SAST examines all the possible ways a piece of software could run, including edge cases that rarely occur in practice. For example, this can show vulnerabilities whether the data is entered by a user, comes in through a database, or comes in from an application programming interface (API).

SAST is best used by integrating it into the build environment. This allows developers to detect vulnerabilities early, while the application is still under development, and it helps ensure that all of the application code is examined.

Recent extensions of SAST allow it to be part of an integrated development environment (IDE), where spellchecker-like testing can give immediate feedback as code is written.

# Compliance

This section contains a set of terms related to compliance with government regulations and industry standards and regulations as well as a set of terms that represent some of the forces driving those standards and other industry best practices.

The core of this section is the *confidentiality, integrity, and availability (CIA) security triad*. These three principles drive the best practices, standards, and regulations that organizations should – and in the case of regulations must – comply with.

Compliance may seem like an unnecessary burden imposed by an outside group, something you must do before you can proceed with your "real" work. However, to paraphrase an old saying, "if you think compliance is expensive, compare it to the cost of a security breach." When you consider that a security breach can expose your company to legal actions, damage its finances and reputation, and even threaten its viability, it is easier to see compliance as a critical strategic management tool.

Your business success depends on the trust of your customers, investors, and employees. A breach can destroy that trust. Compliance cannot guarantee that you won't suffer a security breach, but a breach that occurs because you did not comply with standards or regulations can be much more damaging. In particular, some standards and regulations, including *PCI DSS* and *HIPAA*, provide safe harbor provisions that can shield you from some legal actions. However, these provisions require compliance with the applicable standard or regulation, and non-compliance is likely to result in devastating legal consequences.

The most important new development in compliance is the *General Data Protection Regulation (GDPR)* from the European Union. In addition to addressing issues of privacy, the regulation also creates requirements related to cybersecurity in general. Here are some of those requirements:

- Ensure that you appropriately secure all personal information
- Develop the ability to restore access to personal information after an event
- Monitor and test your systems to ensure compliance with the regulation
- Report a breach to appropriate authorities within 72 hours
- Report certain breaches to those affected by the event

Compliance is not free. It requires assessments, planning, tracking, training, and documentation. Because standards and regulations change, it's important to work closely with a cybersecurity specialist to ensure that your processes and business practices are up to date.

Following best practices, implementing standards, and complying with regulations will not guarantee security; nothing does. However, compliance with cybersecurity standards and regulations can reduce the likelihood of security breaches and help diminish the impact when they occur.

Terms in this section:

- Confidentiality
- Integrity
- Availability
- Separation of Duties
- Policy
- Standard
- Regulation
- Privacy
- Controls
- Payment Card Industry Data Security Standard (PCI DSS)
- General Data Protection Regulation (GDPR)

Audrey Gendreau
Confidentiality

What is it?
The safeguarding of data from unauthorized access or disclosure.

Why is it important?
Confidentiality is part of the *confidentiality, integrity, and availability (CIA) security triad.* In the CIA security model, the objective of confidentiality is to prevent the disclosure of information to unauthorized entities.

About Audrey Gendreau

Audrey Gendreau, PhD, Certified Information Systems Security Professional (CISSP), and Global Information Assurance Certified Forensic Examiner (GCFE), is a security analyst in the retail industry with a background in university-level research and teaching. A frequent presenter at international conferences, her publications have focused on intrusion detection and the Internet of Things. Audrey is a coach and mentor for the Air Force Association CyberPatriot program, which inspires K-12 students in the US to prepare for careers in science and technology.

Email   audreygendreau@icloud.com
Website   researchgate.net/profile/Audrey_Gendreau
LinkedIn   linkedin.com/in/audrey-gendreau-148806a

Why does a business professional need to know this?

Confidentiality is a fundamental concept of information security that business professionals, as well as cybersecurity professionals, must understand. After information is collected or generated, it must be evaluated and assigned a level of security appropriate to company policy and other regulatory controls. Maintaining confidentiality in accordance with the security level assigned by the organization is a responsibility of all business professionals.

The question of data confidentiality gained media attention when Edward Snowden disclosed NSA documents in 2013, revealing data collected by the U.S. government's internet and phone surveillance program [32][30]. The issue in this case was whether Snowden was acting as a whistleblower when he disclosed these documents and whether acting as a whistleblower justified the release of these documents, despite their level of confidentiality.

Regulatory legislation and standards to protect personal information exist at all levels from international standards to local laws. Examples include the following:

- US: Health Insurance Portability and Accountability Act (HIPAA)[148]
- EU: General Data Protection Regulation (GDPR)[27]
- Industry: Payment Card Industry Data Security Standard (PCI DSS)[149]
- US: Children's Online Privacy Protection Act (COPPA)[28].
- California: Shine the Light Law[29]

Once information is classified, organizations use employee education (for example, password complexity guidelines) and technical controls to protect confidentiality. Technical controls include: secure protocols, encryption, password protection, *firewalls*, and *antivirus* mechanisms.

To design a secure infrastructure, companies must provide safeguards against unauthorized access and maintain the confidentiality of information assets as mandated by both the relevant regulatory bodies and business policy.

Daniel Ziesmer
Integrity

What is it?

An assurance that information remains unaltered from its intended state as it is produced, transmitted, stored, and received. Ensuring integrity may include ensuring the non-repudiation and authenticity of information as well.

Why is it important?

Integrity is considered by many to be the most important element of the *confidentiality, integrity, and availability (CIA) security triad*. Any system that is otherwise *available* and *confidential* can still be rendered useless if a user cannot be confident that the information it contains is trustworthy, accurate, and complete.

About Daniel Ziesmer

Daniel Ziesmer is the president of Centripetum, LLC, a Governance, Risk Management, and Compliance (GRC) consulting firm that supports small business risk management and cybersecurity efforts. He is a former professor, security architect, and compliance professional who has established security programs for complex IT and industrial control system environments. Daniel holds numerous industry certifications, is a contributor to a number of scientific and security organizations, and has served as technical editor for more than a dozen industry books and textbooks.

Email	integrity@centripetum.com
Website	centripetum.com
Twitter	@Centripetum
LinkedIn	linkedin.com/company/centripetum
Facebook	facebook.com/centripetum

Why does a business professional need to know this?

If you can alter information, you can alter the decisions people make using that information. For organizations, information is of little use unless they can be assured of its integrity. Therefore, maintaining information and system integrity is a core objective of today's cybersecurity efforts.

Integrity concerns have existed since the earliest days of computing, when system designers used cyclic redundancy checks (CRC) to detect and address errors in data transmission and storage components. While the kind of physical integrity check that CRC provides remains important, cybersecurity predominantly addresses logical integrity of information and the accidental, deliberate, and unauthorized actions that may compromise integrity.

Protections for integrity generally operate at the information and system levels. At the information level, controls are applied to the actual information and its processing, transfer, and storage. At the system level, controls ensure the system can operate unimpaired, while preventing and detecting unauthorized manipulations or integrity violations that could lead to information compromise, theft/*exfiltration* of data, business disruption, reputational damage, etc.

Integrity assurance is a part of most security controls implemented and used today. Examples include the following:

- **Patching:** improving processing integrity so exploits cannot compromise coding weaknesses
- **Antivirus:** defending against code designed to compromise the integrity of systems and information
- **File/container permissions:** defining the scope of who and what actions can be taken
- **Backups and version control:** preserving original copies to defend against unauthorized changes
- **Encryption and digital signing:** ensuring information cannot be stolen (encryption) or altered (digital signing)
- **Detection controls:** logging, monitoring, and intrusion detection systems (IDS) to discover unauthorized system modifications

Michael Moorman
Availability

What is it?
An assurance that information can be requested by and delivered to authorized individuals whenever required.

Why is it important?
Availability is part of the *confidentiality, integrity, and availability (CIA) security triad*. Even if information is kept confidential and has integrity, it still must be available so that authorized individuals can access the information in a reasonable period of time.

About Michael Moorman
Michael Moorman has been a full-time faculty member at Saint Leo University for 27 years, teaching computer information systems, computer science, and cybersecurity courses. He is a member of the IEEE Computer Society, a senior member of the ACM, and a Certified Information Systems Security Professional (CISSP). Prior to earning his doctorate and becoming a professor, he served in the US Air Force as a pilot and engineer.

Email   Michael.Moorman@saintleo.edu

Why does a business professional need to know this?

A business professional needs to understand availability because it constitutes one leg of the confidentiality, integrity, availability (CIA) security triad, which is the foundation of secure information in cybersecurity.

Your efforts to secure your systems and data mean nothing if that data is not available to authorized users (individuals or other systems). Availability can be compromised by malicious individuals or by accident in many ways, including the following:

- *Distributed Denial of Service (DDoS) attacks*, which attempt to slow down or crash systems by flooding a system with requests from many different systems
- Malicious software that either crashes or slows down a system
- System slow downs or crashes caused by malicious *insiders* or human error
- Unexpectedly high volume of legitimate requests (e.g., a popular item goes on sale)

To help ensure availability, organizations need to plan for peak usage, for example by using load balancing and fail-over strategies. They also need to follow best practices for creating a strong cybersecurity defense. These include *vulnerability assessments*, *business continuity planning*, and *incident response planning*.

While these practices are not inexpensive, consider the loss in sales and productivity if your systems and data were to become unavailable for an extended period of time.

Ron LaPedis
Separation of Duties

What is it?

A strategy that helps reduce fraud and error by assigning two or more parts of a transaction to separate individuals. For example, the same person should not be able to enter an invoice then approve payment.

Why is it important?

Separation of duties (SoD) (also known as segregation of duties) prevents the same person from performing two or more parts of a transaction that would be susceptible to error or fraud if performed by one person. Fraud perpetrated through the lack of internal controls can lead to the loss of money, reputation, and market share as well as risking fines from regulators and, perhaps ultimately, shutdown of the organization.

About Ron LaPedis

Ron LaPedis is a global enablement specialist with Micro Focus, focusing on identity, access, and security. He is a prolific author, blogger, and speaker with more than 21 years of information security, business continuity, and emergency response experience. Ron is also a Distinguished Fellow of the Ponemon Institute and a member of the Responsible Information Management (RIM) council.

Email	rlapedis@seacliffpartners.com
Twitter	@RLaPedis_MCRO

Why does a business professional need to know this?

In its 2017 annual report, power and robotics firm ABB Robotics said losses from fraud at its South Korean unit would total $73 million. Managers failed to maintain sufficient segregation of duties in its treasury unit and failed to keep the signature seals (used in many Asian countries) secure, allowing a single employee to bind the company to unauthorized financial contracts[122].

In a 2016 case, an employee of a federal credit union embezzled $1,945,000 from her employer over a 15-year period by removing cash from the vault and placing it in her purse. She deposited some of the cash into credit union accounts she controlled and took the remainder of it for personal expenses. She manipulated the credit union's books and records to cover up her crime[125].

In both of these cases, appropriate separation of duties could have stopped the fraudulent activities. Appropriate separation of duties requires measures such as the following:

- One person to enter an invoice and a second to approve payment
- One person to receive and log a payment, another to deposit it, and a third to reconcile payments against deposits
- Two signatures on a check
- Two keys to a safe deposit box
- Two passwords to approve an electronic funds transfer
- One person to create or update content, another to edit, and a third to approve for publication

In many Asian countries, a seal or chop is the accepted way of signing a contract on behalf of a company. If separation of duties is properly implemented, using a seal would require two people to access the seal, using a dual-key or dual-combination safe, and two people to witness and sign off on any document on which the seal was used.

One person should never be able to remove cash from a vault and then update paper and electronic records to cover up his or her tracks. Whenever money is moved, there should be at least two people involved to help prevent fraud due to lack of SoD controls.

Rodney Richardson
Policy

What is it?
A set of mandatory requirements that apply to specific areas of an organization's operations, including cybersecurity.

Why is it important?
Policies are important because they define the strategic intent for rules, regulations, protocols, and procedures that the organization or industry implement.

About Rodney Richardson
Rodney Richardson has offered senior risk management expertise in leadership positions at some of the top financial institutions in the world. He is currently a vice president in the Group Audit division at Deutsche Bank, focusing on cybersecurity. Rodney was a vice president on the Strategy, Planning, and Governance team at Citigroup and also served as global head of security technology management at BNY Mellon.

Email   r.richardson90@yahoo.com
LinkedIn   linkedin.com/in/rodney-richardson-cism-2285307

Why does a business professional need to know this?

Without effective policies, governance becomes challenging – if not impossible.

Writing effective information security policies requires knowledge of a broad range of issues that might affect your organization. Concise policies, written in simple and unambiguous language, are more likely to be read, understood, and followed. Policies should cover how to track compliance, how to handle exceptions, and the consequences for not complying with the policy.

Research for writing effective policies must include exploration of relevant legal considerations.

Policies adopted by the executive body within an organization need reinforcement in the form of guidelines, procedures, and protocols on how the policies are to be implemented.

Business professionals need to ensure that corporate policies support an information security management strategy that guides cybersecurity specialists in the right direction to secure the organization's information. If your cybersecurity specialists do not understand these mandates, they are likely to overlook management requirements.

Ulf Mattsson
Standards

What is it?
A common set of rules designed to ensure interoperability between different products, systems, and organizations.

Why is it important?
Standards provide stable, long-term guidelines that products can be validated against to ensure they will operate correctly and securely with other products that adhere to the same standard. Standards reflect the best practices of experienced cybersecurity professionals.

About Ulf Mattsson
Ulf Mattsson is the chief technology officer at Atlantic BT Security Solutions and earlier at Compliance Engineering. He was the chief technology officer and a founder of Protegrity. Prior to Protegrity, Ulf worked for 20 years at IBM in software development. He holds more than 50 patents and has worked in standards bodies, including ANSI X9 and PCI DSS. Leading journals and professions magazines have published more than 100 of his in-depth professional papers.

Email	ulf.mattsson@atlanticbt.com
Website	atlanticbt.com/services/cybersecurity
LinkedIn	linkedin.com/in/umattsson

Why does a business professional need to know this?

Business professionals must decide which standards make business sense for their companies to implement. In the area of cybersecurity, the National Institute for Science and Technology Cybersecurity Framework (NIST CSF)[2] is the most widely used framework for cybersecurity.

Other important security standards and standards organizations include the following:

- **ISO/IEC 27001 and 27002:** information security management systems[138]
- **Consortium for IT Software Quality (CISQ):** develops standards related to software quality[139]
- **Information Security Forum (ISF):** publishes the Standard of Good Practice[140]
- **ISO 15408:** standards for computer security certification, also known as Common Criteria[141]
- **Payment Card Industry Data Security Standard (PCI DSS):** standard for handling credit and debit card data and transactions[149]
- **Federal Information Processing Standards (FIPS):** series of standards for cryptography and US federal standards for government systems[142]

Some standards, for example *PCI DSS*, are mandated by industry to ensure a high level of security across multiple participants. If you want to process credit and debit cards, you must follow PCI DSS or partner with a processor who complies with that standard. Other standards are based on industry best practices that have been shown to improve security.

Vanessa Harrison
Regulation

What is it?
A set of rules, usually backed by a legal mandate, that control an activity or environment and provide a means for compliance to be inspected and enforced.

Why is it important?
The internet is an ever-changing environment where the rules are constantly being amended and updated as new technologies emerge. Regulations attempt to control the technological environment and the human behavior associated with it.

About Vanessa Harrison
Vanessa Harrison, BA (Hons), CELTA, DELTA, MBA, MSc, is a management systems consultant, course writer and associate tutor for the British Standards Institution (BSI) in the EMEA region. She specializes in ISO 27001, ISO 22301, ISO 31000, and ISO 9001. Vanessa implements and audits the aforementioned standards and teaches the same at all levels, including the lead implementer and lead auditor qualifications. She is also a Cyber Essentials practitioner and a BSI committee member for the ISO 31000 standard.

Email	vanessa.harrison@hatseu.com
LinkedIn	linkedin.com/in/vanessa-harrison-ba-hons-celta-delta-mba-msc-a9868b14

Why does a business professional need to know this?

The internet, being a relatively new and rapidly evolving environment, has been perceived as inherently devoid of control in its creation and, therefore, a space of perceived freedom. Freedom and control can be seen in both positive and negative lights. They present a double-edged sword; controlled environments may actually allow for more freedom, whereas free environments may encourage a lack of control and, therefore, chaos. The existence (or lack) of safety and security is a preoccupation for many, both personally and professionally.

In reality, the web environment has always been subject to control. There are many ways to regulate an environment: by law, through social norms, through market forces, or by imposing physical and logical constraints. Each of these has been applied to the internet.

In a business context, it is important to understand what is behind the setting of new rules and norms online and to know how those changes will affect us, either directly or indirectly[112]. Of course, as business professionals, we need to be prepared for new political, environmental, sociological, technological, legal, and economic factors that might have an impact on our organization. We must be prepared to adjust our business practices to react to new regulations related to cybersecurity.

Jay Beta
Privacy

What is it?

The concept that individuals own all of their personal information and have sole authority over who should have access to their information and how, when, and where it can be distributed.

Why is it important?

All organizations that deal with private health information in the US must abide by the Health Insurance Portability and Accountability Act (HIPAA)[148]. In addition, the European Union's *General Data Protection Regulation (GDPR)* legislation affects all organizations that deal with people in the European Union, regardless of where the organization is based. To abide by the law and to respond to customer needs, business professionals must take privacy seriously.

About Jay Beta

Jay Beta, MBA, Certified Information Systems Auditor (CISA), Certified in Risk and Information Systems Control (CRISC) , Certified Information Security Manager (CISM), and Payment Card Industry Professional (PCIP), has been an information security professional for 16 years in both private- and public-sector roles. He has extensive background in leadership along with IT compliance, auditing, risk management, governance, and security engineering. He currently works as a cybersecurity executive for a national financial institution.

Email   jasonbeta@gmail.com
LinkedIn   linkedin.com/in/jasonbeta

Why does a business professional need to know this?

Privacy is becoming ever more important as organizations collect, analyze, process, and archive large amounts of information about individuals. Personal information is collected by many organizations, including financial institutions, credit agencies, and governments.

Securing private information is one of the greatest challenges of the internet era. As cybersecurity breaches become more frequent, the entities collecting and storing personal information are at risk of unintentionally exposing private data. The Equifax breach of 2017 exposed the private data of 148 million Americans[38]. Once private information is exposed, it can result in a permanent loss of privacy for the affected individuals.

Privacy considerations are global in nature. The European Union has enacted the General Data Protection Regulation (GDPR)[27], which addresses the concerns of people in the EU around loss of privacy. While no equivalent legislation exists in the US, some elements of the US Constitution have been applied to provide protections for some aspects of privacy. In addition, federal statutes, such as the Health Insurance Portability and Accountability Act (HIPAA)[148], have been enacted to protect information in specific areas.

There is evidence to suggest that a generational difference exists on the question of what exactly is privacy and what should (and should not) be private. Many people agree that at least some information should be kept confidential and in the sole possession of the information owner. However, younger people are believed to be more open to sharing personal details on social media platforms. This may help to explain why the US Federal Trade Commission says younger "digital native" consumers are "more vulnerable" to scams and more likely than any other group to have lost money to fraud[103].

At the same time, older users tend to be skeptical about sharing information they perceive as private. The differences between generations lie in what each generation considers private information. Business professionals need to understand these differences and respect both the privacy concerns of their customers and the regulations under which their organizations operate.

Mark Sears
Controls

What is it?

A set of guidelines designed to protect an organization's information security, safeguarding the standards of *confidentiality, integrity, and availability (CIA)*.

Why is it important?

Controls are important because without them, an organization has no guidelines for protecting information and assets.

About Mark Sears

Mark Sears, a senior systems engineer with Assured Information Technology in Orlando, FL, has been working in cybersecurity for over 10 years for Fortune 200 companies, including Lockheed Martin and General Dynamics. Mark has a BA in communications from Loyola University, an MS in technology management from Rensselaer Polytechnic Institute, and an MS in information assurance from Norwich University. His professional certifications include Certified Information Systems Security Professional (CISSP) and Microsoft Certified Solutions Expert (MCSE).

Email	marksears418@gmail.com
LinkedIn	linkedin.com/in/mark-s-b731a352

Why does a business professional need to know this?

The primary cybersecurity function is to protect data, which includes keeping people who should not have access away from data (*confidentiality*), ensuring that data is not altered by unauthorized entities (*integrity*), and maintaining an environment that makes data accessible when it is needed (*availability*).

Cybersecurity controls provide guidance to specialists, helping them protect the security environment. These controls fall into various categories, including the following:

- **Physical:** the organization must provide locks on doors
- **Technical:** users must use passwords to access systems
- **Regulatory/legal:** the authorities must be notified if a breach is detected

As part of the process of protecting an organization's data, an analyst uses a checklist of controls to ensure that proper security measures are applied so that only authorized persons or processes have access to the organization's data and assets.

These controls are developed mainly by government entities such as the US National Institute of Standards and Technology (NIST). NIST has developed the Risk Management Framework (RMF)[2], a roadmap for an organization to follow to properly secure its cybersecurity stance[33]. The RMF asks cybersecurity specialists to assign risk based on the type of system to be secured (i.e., a larger network connected to the internet or a smaller, disconnected stand-alone network). The larger, connected network would have more or different controls applied, since there is more risk of a breach. The disconnected network, while still needing protection, would require less stringent controls[34].

John Elliott
Payment Card Industry Data Security Standard (PCI DSS)

What is it?
A prescriptive information security standard designed to protect the confidentiality of credit and debit card data.

Why is it important?
All organizations that store, process, or transmit payment card data typically have a contractual requirement to comply with PCI DSS. Some countries and US states also mandate PCI DSS compliance by law[84].

About John Elliott
John Elliott helps organizations balance risk and regulation with business needs. He is a specialist in payments (John contributed to the development of many PCI standards, including PCI DSS), privacy, and cybersecurity. A passionate and innovative communicator, he presents frequently at conferences, online, and in boardrooms.

John is a chartered fellow of the British Computer Society (BCS), holds professional certifications in risk, privacy and security, and is a Pluralsight Author.

Website	withoutfire.com
Twitter	@withoutfire
LinkedIn	uk.linkedin.com/in/withoutfire

Why does a business professional need to know this?

Organizations that store, process, or transmit credit or debit card data must balance PCI DSS requirements with their own cybersecurity assessment – in some cases, they may chose to outsource or segment their processing and apply PCI DSS to only a sub-set of their systems. Such organizations have two aims: to be secure and to comply with PCI DSS. An unhealthy balance between these two can lead to a "compliance first" culture, jeopardizing the organization's cybersecurity.

PCI DSS is a prescriptive security standard consisting of twelve major security requirements (e.g. install and maintain a firewall configuration to protect cardholder data) broken down into around 280 sub-requirements. The requirements apply to all systems, processes, and people that store, process, or transmit cardholder data (known as the cardholder data environment or CDE) and all systems connected to the CDE.

Merchants that accept payment cards must formally validate their PCI DSS compliance to their acquiring merchant bank annually by undergoing an external audit or by completing a self-assessment. Service providers to merchants and financial institutions also must validate their compliance annually[85][86].

Organizations subject to PCI DSS typically segment their networks and systems into those parts that have to comply with PCI DSS and those that do not. Some organizations outsource operations that require PCI DSS compliance to vendors such as PayPal. The reason for this is that PCI DSS has much more stringent cybersecurity requirements than are necessary for systems that do not handle such sensitive data. Reducing the number of systems that must comply with PCI DSS also allows organizations to focus their compliance efforts on a smaller number of systems.

Organizations that suffer a breach in confidentiality of payment card data will receive *safe harbor* from card scheme financial penalties if the organization was PCI DSS compliant at the time of the breach.

Regine Bonneau
General Data Protection Regulation (GDPR)

What is it?

A European Union regulation designed to give people more control over their personal data and to define how organizations must process such data.

Why is it important?

The GDPR expands the scope of data protection globally. This is important because it applies to many more organizations than previous regulations. In particular, the GDPR applies to any entity that has an establishment (any place of business) in the European Union and collects or processes personal data about any person in the world. And it applies to any entity that collects or processes personal data from a person in the European Union, regardless of where that entity is based.

About Regine Bonneau

Regine Bonneau is a leading expert on cybersecurity, governance, risk management, and compliance. Her career spans 20 years with a focus on technology and processes in the healthcare, financial, legal, and energy sectors. Ms. Bonneau is the founder of RB Advisory, LLC, which provides cyber risk management, security assessments, compliance services, forensic audits, and privacy consultations for private-sector and government clients. She is a sought-after speaker and holds leadership roles in several technology industry associations.

Email	rbonneau@rbadvisoryllc.com
Website	rbadvisoryllc.com
Twitter	@luderbonneau
LinkedIn	linkedin.com/in/regine-bonneau-ctprp-22500824
Facebook	facebook.com/regine.bonneau.5

Why does a business professional need to know this?

The EU GDPR is the most significant change in data privacy regulation in the European Union since 1995[49]. It affects the overall risk and security management processes of any company that collects or processes information from a person in the European Union. Business professionals worldwide, not just in the EU, need to deal with the GDPR.

Key elements of the GDPR, which became effective in May 2018, include the following:

- **Territorial scope:** GDPR applies to all companies in the EU and overseas that do business with citizens of the EU, regardless of whether their data processing occurs in the EU or elsewhere.
- **Penalties:** Organizations that breach the GDPR can be fined up to the greater of 4% of annual global turnover or €20 Million.
- **Consent:** The GDPR requires terms and conditions related to personal data to be clear and free of unintelligible terms and legalese.
- **Data breach notification:** Any breach must be reported to authorities within 72 hours.
- **Right to access:** Consumers have the right to know what their data is being used for and to receive a copy of their data.
- **Right to be forgotten:** Also known as the "right to erasure," this says that consumers may request that their data be erased. This right comes with some qualifications.
- **Data portability:** Consumers can access their data and send it to another company, again with some qualifications.
- **Data Protection Officers and Privacy Impact Assessment:** Organizations that engage in large-scale monitoring or processing of sensitive personal data, or which are public authorities, must have a single person responsible for compliance.

The GDPR represents a major change to the way that personal data must be handled. All companies, worldwide, should look closely at their operations; there are provisions in the GDPR that, if not carefully followed, could lead to steep fines. All organizations need to conduct a comprehensive audit to ensure that they collect, store, manage, and use personal data in accordance with the GDPR.

Glossary of Security Terms

This glossary contains a set of definitions that support the terms in the book. The terms here include technical terms, such as exfiltration and HTTPS, and supporting terms, such as authentication and spyware.

Some of these terms will be of interest primarily to security practitioners, but business professionals can find it useful to have at least a high-level understanding of them in case they come up in conversations with practitioners.

About Debra Baker

Debra Baker, Certified Information Systems Security Professional (CISSP), has worked in IT security for 20+ years. Her cybersecurity career began in the US Air Force. She also worked as a public-key infrastructure (PKI) consultant at Entrust Technologies. Currently she works as a product certifications engineer at Cisco specializing in Common Criteria and FIPS Certifications. She is the founder of the Johns Hopkins Cryptographic Knowledge Base, which conveys cryptography in a practical manner for IT administrators, developers, and managers.

Email	debinfosec@gmail.com
Website	debinfosec.com
Twitter	@deb_infosec
LinkedIn	linkedin.com/in/debrabakernc

adware

Software that generates online advertisements. Adware can be a form of *malware* if the advertisements are unwanted or appear as a window or pop-up that can't be closed.

anti-malware signature

See *malware signature*

antivirus

Software designed to detect and remove computer viruses. Modern antivirus software also provides protection against other types of *malware*, including *adware*, *ransomware*, *spyware*, and other threats.

assurance

A process by which a product, process, or implementation is verified by a third-party *auditor* and/or by testing to ensure that a stated policy is being met.

asymmetric-key cryptography

See *public-key cryptography*.

attack surface

The set of points (aka *attack vectors*) in a computing environment where an attacker might try to breach security.

attack vector

The manner in which an attacker attempts to violate security. Examples include exploiting *zero-day vulnerabilities*, tricking users into revealing credentials, and exploiting weak passwords.

Attack vectors are typically characterized in two dimensions: level of risk – how much damage could it cause – and ease of attack – how vulnerable the system is to this type of attack. Understanding these dimensions can help business professionals and cybersecurity specialists determine what preventative measures need to be taken.

backdoor

A method for bypassing normal security authentication to gain access to a system. Backdoors can be created for legitimate means, such as helping users retrieve lost passwords or for debugging, but some are created to enable surreptitious access. Backdoors can also be created through malware attached to plugins for software, such as WordPress or Joomla, that supports extensions using plugins.

backups

Data copied to an archive so it can be accessed at a later time if a system has a failure that causes it to lose data.

bitcoin

A digital currency (also known as cryptocurrency) that is independent of a bank or other administrator. Bitcoin uses *blockchain* technology to encrypt a chain of transactions in such a way that those transactions are secure and valid.

black hat

by Taylor Stafford

Hackers who operate with malicious intent, generally conducting their activities to seek personal gain.

blockchain

by Christopher Carfi

A shared ledger technology, based on open protocols, that is the foundation for *Bitcoin*, Ethereum smart contracts, and a number of cryptocurrencies. Blockchain is a new fundamental technology that may end up being as far-reaching as the internet itself. Blockchain is a new way of sharing and storing information that can be used as a store of value as well. In addition to being the basis for cryptocurrencies, blockchains can be used to implement smart contracts and have other novel uses as well.

certification

Certification can mean different things in cybersecurity. Cybersecurity experts can study, pass an exam, and acquire a certification that assesses their background and qualifications. The cybersecurity industry has dozens of certifications issued by several different organizations. Also referred to as *credentials*. Products can be certified after going through a process that evaluates certain qualities of that product. For example, Common Criteria[141] is an international certification that evaluates the security functions of a product.

CIA

See *confidentiality, integrity, and availability (CIA) triad*

classification

In the US military, data is classified into categories such as Top Secret, Secret, and Confidential. Corporations also classify data into categories based on value and importance.

clearnet

The portion of the internet accessible through normal browsers. Distinct from the *dark web*, which is accessible only using specialized software.

click fraud

A type of fraud perpetrated on advertisers who use a pay-per-click model to pay for advertising. Perpetrators repeatedly click on an ad, sometimes using a computer program to automate the procedure, emulating a user. The practice fraudulently increases the revenue generated by the ad. Sometimes click fraud comes from sites that want to increase their ad revenue dishonestly. Other instances include malicious attacks against an advertiser by competitors or people who have motives such as a personal or political grievance.

confidentiality, integrity, and availability (CIA)

by Michael Moorman

The confidentiality, integrity, and availability (CIA) security triad is the foundation of secure information in cybersecurity. These three qualities help ensure that information is kept secure from access by unauthorized individuals (*confidentiality*), has not been modified in storage or in transit (*integrity*), and is accessible to authorized individuals when required (*availability*). None of these three stands alone, but together they form a strong foundation for ensuring information security.

Common Criteria (CC)

The ISO 15408 standard[141]. Common Criteria (CC) defines a set of cybersecurity criteria for product *certification*. A group of member nations has agreed to accept CC certifications performed by any one of a group of authorizing nations. If your product is certified under CC in one of the authorizing nations, then all of the other member nations will recognize and accept that certification. The National Information Assurance Partnership (NIAP) is responsible for implementation of Common Criteria in the US.

credentials

A *certification* or document, typically backed up by some authority, that identifies the holder as having certain qualities. In cybersecurity, credentials can also refer to various means, such as passwords or *biometrics*, used to gain access to a system.

cryptography

by Dennis Charlebois

A method for converting (encrypting) *plaintext* into private ciphertext and back into plaintext (decrypting). See also *public-key encryption* and *private-key encryption*

cyclic redundancy check (CRC)

An error-detecting code that can be used to detect changes in a block of data as it is transmitted. A CRC works by performing a mathematical calculation on a block of data and generating a fixed length code, which is attached to the end of the block. When the block is received, the receiver runs the same calculation and compares the result with the attached code. If they don't match, then there was a change to the data during transmission.

darknet

A part of the addressable internet that has no active hosts. This term is frequently used as a synonym for the *dark web*, though some experts continue to make a distinction.

deep web

Parts of the internet that are not accessible to search engines. The deep web includes content behind paywalls as well as content that is intentionally hidden, such as sites in the *dark web*. In practice, the distinctions between deep web, dark web, and darknet are mostly of interest to specialists.

detection controls

Logging, monitoring, and intrusion detection systems to discover unauthorized system modifications.

digital certificate

A *public-key cryptography*-based method used to prove ownership, typically ownership of a website or domain. Digital certificates can be generated by anyone, but to be useful for proving ownership, they are usually issued through a certificate authority, a company that uses various means to ensure that the party they issue a certificate to is who it says it is. When you use *HTTPS* to access a web site, a modern browser will check the certificate offered by the website, and if that certificate is valid, the browser will display a lock icon, the word secure, or some other indication that it has validated the identity of the website.

digital signature

A means for electronically associating a signer with a document in a transaction using *public-key cryptography*. The broader term electronic signature includes a wide variety of methods with varying levels of assurance and varying levels of acceptance by governments and organizations.

disaster recovery plan

A documented process to recover after a disaster. A disaster recovery plan needs to encompass both man-made and natural disasters, and damage to physical and computing infrastructure, staff, and other resources. A disaster recovery plan is typically part of an organization's *business continuity plan*.

distributed denial-of-service (DDoS) attack

An attack where multiple computers – sometimes thousands spread across the world – target a system or network with a flood of requests. The intent is to shutdown or severely hamper the operation of the target. Attackers often use *botnets* to carry out such attacks.

exfiltration

In cybersecurity, the extraction of data from a computer system without permission.

exploit

An attempt to take advantage of a computer flaw in order to gain unauthorized access to a computer's data.

hacker

A computer expert who solves a problem using technical skills. This includes people who use their skills for either good or bad ends, although in popular culture, the term is most often associated with someone who is trying to break into a computer system without the permission of the owner. Hackers who use their skills for legitimate ends are called *white-hat* hackers, and those who use their skill for malicious purposes are called *black-hat* hackers.

hash function
by Luis Brown

A one-way encryption algorithm used to create a single unique value based on a given data item such as a password or document. Hash functions are used to create a small numerical value from a larger data item. That value has a high probability of being unique for that data item, which means you can compare hash values to see if data items are identical.

HIPAA

The Health Insurance Portability and Accountability Act. A US law that protects medical information. It applies to health care providers, health insurance companies, and others who have to deal with personal health information.

HTTPS

A protocol for secure data transmission used on the internet. HTTPS provides an encrypted path for data between a web service and a user (typically a web browser). Initially, HTTPS was used primarily for payments and other sensitive transactions. However, it is now becoming more common and is likely to soon surpass the original HTTP protocol in terms of usage.

I2P

The Invisible Internet Project. I2P is a network layer that supports anonymous communication. It runs on a network of 55,000 computers (run by volunteers) that routes messages in such a way that it is hard for a third party to trace a connection. I2P is used for private communication and also to connect to the *dark web*. See also *Tor*.

IDE

Integrated Development Environment. A programming environment that typically provides a graphical user interface (GUI) for programmers, with tools such as editors, debuggers, and testing software.

indicators of compromise (IOC)

IOCs are characteristics of malware that can be used to develop anti-malware signatures, patches to address the vulnerabilities being exploited, and threat intelligence to determine where a particular piece of malware fits in a broader cybersecurity attack.

information asset

by Steve Gibson

Any hard copy, digital information, or knowledge that can be classified with a level of importance. Information assets are more than just IT infrastructure; they include personnel, premises, secure working areas, integrated management systems, software systems, and the information itself. These assets should all have defined owners who understand their security implications, the controls needed to protect them, and security risks identified as part of information security risk management.

internet hygiene

A set of practices that help keep you safe on the internet. They include, keeping software up to date, running *antivirus* software, using strong passwords, using two-factor or *multi-factor authentication*, backing up systems, and running a *firewall*.

least privilege

An approach to cybersecurity that follows the principle that a program or person should have the minimum amount of access required to perform their assigned tasks and no more.

malware

A program that is inserted into a system, usually covertly, with the intent of compromising the confidentiality, integrity, or availability of the victim's data, applications, or operating system or of otherwise annoying or disrupting the victim. Malware includes *viruses*, *spyware*, *ransomware*, and other harmful programs.

malware signature

A pattern of data that can be used to detect and identify a particular piece of malware. Analogous to a fingerprint, malware signatures, also known as *virus* signatures or anti-malware signatures, are used by antivirus programs to find malware. When *antivirus* software operates, it scans data looking for blocks of data that match a malware signature. When a match is found, the antivirus software can send an alert or isolate and remove the program that contains the signature.

man-in-the-middle attack

An attack that inserts itself into a data connection and watches traffic. Such an attack can remain undetected by both sides in a communication, collecting information or fooling one party in the connection into revealing sensitive information.

onion routing

A method for routing information on a network that encrypts address information so that each node in the transmission only knows about the immediately preceding and following nodes, but does not know the ultimate destination of the transmission. Onion routing uses *public-key encryption* to create layers of addresses, each of which can be read only by certain nodes. Thus, no node can determine the complete route.

patching

The process of applying updates to software to fix or improve it. Software vendors use patches to keep customer systems up to date and as secure as possible. End users should apply the latest available patches to their software.

permissions

A set of properties that define the scope of who may access a resource (file, network connection, etc.) and what actions can be taken on the resource (read, write, create, delete, etc.).

personally identifiable information (PII)

by Kathy Stershic

Data that on its own or in combination with other data can identify a specific person. PII is a legal term that carries specific implications and obligations, and the handling (or mishandling) of personal information can have a profound impact on a company's brand and reputation. Also known as sensitive personal information (SPI).

Petya

A variety of encrypting *ransomware* malware that was first encountered in 2016. It was propagated through email attachments. Petya targets Microsoft Windows systems, encrypting the system's hard drive, preventing the system from booting until the victim pays a ransom and receives a decryption key.

plaintext

Unencrypted information. Typically includes human-readable text, but can also include binary files that can be viewed without using decryption software.

potentially unwanted program (PUP)

Software that users may not want to have on their system. This can include programs that inject ads, hijack browsers, or track user activities. PUPs often come inside other, legitimate, software packages or as part of downloads.

private-key cryptography

by Michael Melone

An encryption method that uses a single private key, password, or passphrase to encrypt and decrypt messages. This message requires both parties to a communication to hold the same key and keep it private. Because the algorithms that implement private-key encryption are typically faster than those that implement *public-key encryption*, systems often will use public-key encryption to initiate a conversation, then share a one-time-use private key for the rest of the communication. Also known as symmetric-key cryptography.

protected health information

by Frank DiPiazza

Under US Law, this is any information about health status, provision of healthcare, or payment of healthcare provided to a patient from a healthcare provider.

public-key cryptography
by Chris Gida

An encryption method that uses a key pair (one public key and one corresponding private key) for encrypting data. The two keys have a mathematical relationship that ensures that messages encrypted using one key can only be decrypted using the other key. To use public-key cryptography, you generate two keys, a private key that you keep secure and don't share and a public key that can be distributed freely.

Public-key encryption is typically used in two ways. You can authenticate a message as coming from you by encrypting it (or its *hash value*) with your private key. Only your public key can decrypt the message, thus ensuring that if the message can be decrypted, it came from you. And someone can encrypt a message to you using the public key. In that case, only your private key can decrypt the message (or its hash value), making that message only accessible to you. Also known as asymmetric-key cryptography.

role-based access control (RBAC)
A form of access control based on an individual's assigned role and the tasks someone with that role needs to perform. Users are given access based on what permissions are appropriate to complete the tasks the role requires.

safe harbor
Provisions in a regulation or law that protect people from prosecution for violating that law provided they follow certain rules. For example, current US copyright law protects internet service providers from liability for violations by their customers as long as they follow certain requirements.

script kiddie
An unskilled person who uses existing programs to try and hack into computer systems, but has little knowledge of how those programs work.

security triad
See *confidentiality, integrity, and availability (CIA)*.

sensitive personal information (SPI)
See *personally identifiable information (PII)*.

spam

Electronic junk mail or the abuse of electronic messaging systems to indiscriminately send unsolicited bulk messages. Spam typically contains ads or links to *malware*.

spear phishing

A *phishing* attack directed at a specific individual, based on that person's job or personal interests. An organization chart or social media postings (notably Facebook and LinkedIn) can be used to create a spear phishing attack based on personal or professional interests.

spyware

Software that attempts to collect information on a computer system without the user being aware of it. Spyware sometimes gets installed as part of a legitimate software program, with or without the knowledge of the developer of that program. Information collected could include passwords, personal information, or information that can be used to target ads.

SSL/TLS

Cryptographic protocols used to encrypt data traversing a network. SSL is an acronym for Secure Sockets Layer, and TLS is an acronym for Transport Layer Security. SSL and TLS provide authentication, confidentiality, and integrity for communication on the internet.

symmetric-key cryptography

See *private-key cryptography*.

threat actor

A person who poses a threat that affects the security or safety of another person or system. The term is typically used to describe people or groups who act maliciously.

Tor

Software used for anonymous networking. Tor allow users to browse on the internet, send instant messages, and chat. It uses *onion routing* to preserve the anonymity of users. Tor is often used to access the *dark web*. See also *I2P*.

trojan horse

A type of *malware* that misleads a user. A trojan horse might be an email attachment that contains malware or a program that claims to do one thing but also contains malware hidden inside.

version control

A system that archives data so you can access that data as it existed at points in the past. Version control systems allow you to keep a history of the state of your data in case you need to access previous versions.

virtual private network (VPN)

A VPN creates a private, encrypted connection that allows someone to access a private network (for example, an internal corporate) from the public internet. Corporations use VPNs to allow employees to connect with the corporate network while working from home or other locations that are not directly connected to the corporate network. Pople also use VPN services to provide greater protection from threats such as a *man-in-the-middle* attack when they connect to the internet from a public wifi hotspot (e.g., an unencrypted wifi service in a coffee shop or other public place).

virus

A type of malware that modifies the code of another program, inserting its own code and, thus, replicating itself. Viruses can carry *ransomware*, *spyware*, and other forms of *malware*. See also *worm*.

virus signature

See *malware signature*.

WannaCry

A ransomware *worm* that targets Windows systems. WannaCry was first encountered in May 2017 and quickly spread, infecting more than 230,000 systems across 150 countries[108]. See also *Petya*.

watering hole exploit

An attack strategy that targets a group by placing *malware* on a site commonly used by members of the group. The term derives from real-world predators, who often attack prey near a watering hole.

whaling

A *phishing* or *spear phishing* attack that targets high-level executives or other high-profile individuals.

white hat

A cybersecurity expert who uses techniques such as *penetration testing* to do a friendly test of a system for vulnerabilities. Also known as an ethical hacker, white hats are often employed by companies to discover weaknesses in their cybersecurity defenses.

worm

Software that can replicate itself and spread to other computers via a network. A worm is similar to a *virus*, except that a virus must be carried by another program. A worm doesn't need a host program.

zero-day exploit

by James McQuiggan

An exploit that takes advantage of a previously unknown vulnerability (i.e., a *zero-day vulnerability*) to gain access to a system.

zombie

A computer or device that has been infected by a *virus* that allows a hacker to control it remotely. Zombies are typically part of a *botnet* that can be used to carry out *Distributed Denial of Service (DDoS)* attacks, send spam, or store illegal data.

Additional Contributors

The people recognized in this section provided content that we used in the introductions and the glossary for this book. Their contributions to this book provided context for the terms and additional information necessary to provide as full a picture of the current state of cybersecurity as possible.

Luis Brown

Luis Brown began his career as a software developer 35 years ago. After 20 years, he transitioned to information technology leadership. He holds several information security certifications including Certified Information Systems Security Professional (CISSP), Certified Chief Information Security Officer (C|CISO), and Certified Ethical Hacker (C|EH). He currently serves as the CISO for Central New Mexico Community College.

Email   lbrown76@cnm.edu
Website   cnm.edu
LinkedIn   linkedin.com/in/luisbrown

Phil Burton

Phil Burton is a principal consultant and senior trainer for 280 Group. He has worked with US and non-US clients with business-to-business (B2B) products and services covering applications and infrastructure, over the entire product life cycle. Phil's 25-year career working for established companies and startups in Silicon Valley has given him domain expertise in information security, networking, and data communications. Phil is a contributing author to the best-selling book *42 Rules of Product Management* and co-author of *42 Rules of Product Marketing* .

Email   phil@280group.com
Website   280group.com/280-group/team
LinkedIn   linkedin.com/in/philipmburton

Christopher Carfi

Christopher Carfi heads up global content marketing for GoDaddy. Previously, he spent nearly ten years as part of the advanced technology group at Andersen Consulting/Accenture. He has headed up product, marketing, and product marketing groups at a number of early-stage companies and has been a startup founder. Christopher holds a degree in computer science from Northwestern University and an MBA from Carnegie Mellon. He is originally from Chicago and currently lives in Silicon Valley with his family.

Twitter	@ccarfi
LinkedIn	linkedin.com/in/ccarfi

Dennis Charlebois

Dr. Dennis Charlebois is president of d6 Consulting Group, specializing in solving complex technology, business, and marketing problems. Dennis has expertise across security, big data, and the Internet of Things (IoT). Previously, Dennis was vice president and general manager of big data and analytics at Hexis Cyber Solutions. At Cisco, Dennis led strategy and planning for IT security. Prior to Cisco, Dennis was a senior executive at BroadWare Technologies, Certicom (encryption), and DRS Technologies.

Dennis holds a BS in engineering from Carleton University, an MBA from Pepperdine University, and a PhD in executive management from the Peter F. Drucker Graduate Management Center at Claremont Graduate University.

Email	dennisc999@gmail.com
Website	d6group.com
LinkedIn	linkedin.com/in/dr-dennis-charlebois-967b2

Jessica Fernandez

Jessica Fernandez specializes in making the complicated work of securing information simple for the everyday user. She helps employees understand their role in securing information through security training and award-winning awareness campaigns. With a background in marketing and communication, she works to grow internal branding for information security groups, which is pivotal in translating cybersecurity in a way that is engaging and palatable.

Jessica is an independent consultant for the Warner Bros. InfoSec team. Developing thought-provoking awareness campaigns, video content, and eLearning, which included the *Put Yourself in the Picture* and *Superhero Academy* training winners of the learning and InfoSec community awards, Brandon Hall and CSO50.

Email	jessica.fernandez@parleeinc.com

Steve Gibson

Steve Gibson is an information security specialist based in the UK. He has worked in IT for over 15 years, originally managing high volume data processing and production operations before moving to management consultancy, due diligence, and business acquisition.

More recently he has focused on assisting organizations with the challenges of meeting the requirements of new privacy regulations in Europe. Steve now works as an independent data privacy, information, and cybersecurity consultant. He fulfills virtual data privacy and security roles for various organizations, such as chief information security officer (Virtual CISO) and data protection officer (Virtual DPO). He also works with a United Kingdom Accreditation Service (UKAS) accredited certification body to provide ISO27001 and ISO22301 certification audits.

Email	stevegibson@datawebit.com
Website	datawebit.com
Twitter	@DatawebTraining
LinkedIn	uk.linkedin.com/in/datawebinformationsecurity
Facebook	facebook.com/DataWebIT

Chris Gida

Chris Gida has worked in IT and information security for more than ten years. He guides clients in aligning security goals with best practices, regulations, and industry standards, including ISO 27001/2, HIPAA/HITECH, PCI DSS, Risk Management, and VRM. He is a principal security consultant at NCC Group, Chris's experience spans healthcare, retail, education, and manufacturing.

Email	Chris.Gida@nccgroup.trust
Website	nccgroup.trust/us
LinkedIn	linkedin.com/in/christopher-gida-5923498

Guy Helmer

Guy Helmer is a senior lecturer of information systems in the Iowa State University College of Business and distinguished engineer at Absolute Software. Guy lectures on topics of software development, networking, and information security. He develops data security systems across multiple platforms. He received his PhD. in computer science from Iowa State University where he researched network security, high-performance computation, artificial intelligence, and computer architecture.

Email	GHelmer@iastate.edu
Website	business.iastate.edu/faculty/?faculty=ghelmer
Twitter	@ghelmer
LinkedIn	linkedin.com/in/guy-helmer-019b5a1

Matt Kelly

Matt Kelly is an independent compliance consultant who studies corporate compliance, governance, and risk management issues. He maintains a blog, RadicalCompliance.com, where he shares his thoughts on business issues and speaks on compliance, governance, and risk topics frequently.

Kelly was named a "Rising Star of Corporate Governance" by the Millstein Center for Corporate Governance in the inaugural class of 2008, and he was named to Ethisphere's "Most Influential in Business Ethics" list in 2011 (no. 91) and 2013 (no. 77). From 2006 through 2015, Kelly was editor of Compliance Week, a newsletter on corporate compliance.

Email	mkelly@radicalcompliance.com
Website	RadicalCompliance.com
Twitter	@compliancememe
LinkedIn	linkedin.com/in/mkelly1971

Michael Melone

Michael Melone is an information security professional specializing in targeted attack investigation and recovery in the Tampa Bay area. Michael holds a master's degree in information systems and technology management, specializing in information assurance and security. He has been an active (ISC)² Certified Information Systems Security Professional (CISSP) member since 2007 and is the author of the book *Think Like a Hacker: A Sysadmin's Guide to Cybersecurity*. Currently, Michael is a principal consultant within Microsoft's Global Incident Response and Recovery (GIRR) team and performs information security consulting to global organizations in all industry verticals.

Email	michael.melone@bitlatch.com
Website	PersistentAdversary.com
Twitter	@MichaelMelone
LinkedIn	linkedin.com/in/mjmelone
Facebook	facebook.com/meloneit

Taylor Stafford

Taylor Stafford has more than 10 years of experience across consulting, security implementation, and networking for multinational corporations, governments, and the US Department of Defense. His experience includes conducting risk assessments, writing security advisories, authoring policies, and implementing controls. His areas of expertise include information security, risk assessment, and network engineering.

Email	Taylor.Stafford@nccgroup.trust
LinkedIn	linkedin.com/in/taylor-stafford-32518369

Kathy Stershic

Kathy Stershic is principal consultant at Dialog Research & Communications. Serving senior executives in leading-edge IT organizations, her specialty is creating order and driving results in complex environments. In addition to providing strategic research and communication services, Kathy also guides clients on managing data privacy risk through improved organizational practices. A privacy enthusiast, she is a Certified Information Privacy Manager (CIPM) and Certified Information Privacy Professional-US (CIPP/US).

Email	kstershic@dialogrc.com
Website	dialogrc.com
Twitter	@kstershic
LinkedIn	linkedin.com/in/kathystershic

References

We use a link shortener in print because some of the links are extremely long. If you go to https://xmlpress.net/tlocyber/references you will find a list of references with the complete, un-shortened URL for each.

Advanced Persistent Threat by Paul Brager, Jr.

[1] *Anatomy of Advanced Persistent Threats*
https://xplnk.com/vzxoa/
FireEye. Promotional content from FireEye cybersecurity software company that describes advanced persistent threat (APT) attacks and contains a link to a video that illustrates how APTs work.

Application Risk Governance by Graeme Fleck

[2] *Framework for Improving Critical Infrastructure Cybersecurity*
https://www.nist.gov/cyberframework
NIST (2017). A set of voluntary industry standards and best practices designed to help organizations manage cybersecurity risks.

[3] *NIST 800 Publications*
https://xplnk.com/ufhfu/
National Institute of Standards and Technology (NIST), US Department of Commerce, Computer Security Resource Center. A catalog of publications from the Computer Security Division and the Applied Cybersecurity Division of NIST.

[4] *OWASP - Open Web App Security Project*
https://xplnk.com/1o42x/
OWASP (2014). OWASP is an independent open-source body that promotes best practices in software assurance. It is dedicated to enabling organizations to conceive, develop, acquire, operate, and maintain applications that can be trusted.

[5] *United States Computer Emergency Response Team (US-CERT)*
http://www.us-cert.gov/bsi
Best practice articles, knowledge, and tools from the US Computer Emergency Readiness Team, US Department of Homeland Security. A repository of best practices, articles, tools, guidelines, rules, principles, and other resources that software developers, architects, and security practitioners can use to build security into software during each phase of its development.

[6] *DevOps Practitioner Considerations*
https://xplnk.com/cn6wn/
ISACA (2015). PDF. Centralized source of information and guidance in the growing field of auditing controls for computer systems. Registration required.

[7] *Software Assurance: Enabling Security and Resilience throughout the Software Lifecycle*
https://xplnk.com/9cbe1/
Jarzombek, Joe (2012). PDF. Slide deck about software assurance and the need to build security in from the start.

[8] *CIS Controls*
https://www.cisecurity.org/controls
Center for Internet Security.

Audit by Terrie Diaz

[9] *Audit cites town of Geneseo for lax cyber security*
https://xplnk.com/x0sbr/
Leader, Matt (2017). Livingston County News.

Behavioral Monitoring by Holli Harrison

[10] *User entity behavior analytics, next step in security visibility*
https://xplnk.com/f630p/
Zurkus, Kacy (2015). CSO Online.

[11] *Prepare for the Inevitable Security Incident*
https://xplnk.com/4wwlb/
Moore, Susan (2016). Gartner.

Biometrics by Stephen Simchak

[12] *About Those Fingerprints Stolen in the OPM Hack*
https://xplnk.com/rs4le/
Koren, Marina (2015). The Atlantic.

[13] *Inside the Cyberattack That Shocked the US Government*
https://xplnk.com/ubt1o/
Koerner, Brendan (2016). Wired.

[14] *OPM says 5.6 million fingerprints stolen in cyberattack, five times as many as previously thought*
https://xplnk.com/6en4n/
Peterson, Andrea (2015). Washington Post.

Botnet by Tolu Onireti

[15] *Botnet facts*
https://xplnk.com/4f3cg/
Washington State Attorney General. An introduction to botnets, including practical advice on preventing infection and removing malware.

[16] *Bots and Botnets - A growing threat*
https://us.norton.com/botnet/
Symantec. An introduction to botnets and advice on protecting networks from infection.

[17] *What are the best bot detection tools?*
https://xplnk.com/t8qi9/
Skoudis, Ed (2007). TechTarget Security. Introduction to anti-malware tools with a discussion about signature and heuristic detection techniques.

[18] *Botnet in the news - Dyn Analysis summary of Friday October 21st attack*
https://xplnk.com/qm6ml/
Hilton, Scott (2016). Analysis of Distributed Denial of Service attack sustained by cloud infrastructure company, Dyn.

[19] *Inside the Million-Machine Clickfraud Botnet*
https://xplnk.com/9eawz/
Gheorghe, Alexandra (2016). Bitdefender Labs. An introduction to malware and click fraud.

Buffer Overflow Attack by Shawn Connelly

[20] *Intel Management Engine pwned by buffer overflow*
https://xplnk.com/1lmrb/
Claburn, Thomas (2017). The Register. Description of recent flaws in Intel processors that could leave those processors vulnerable to a buffer overflow attack.

[21] *Meltdown and Spectre Patching has been a Total Train Wreck*
https://xplnk.com/2umg6/
Newman, Lily Hay (2018). Wired.

Business Continuity Plan by Dale Shulmistra

[22] *The elements of business continuity planning*
https://xplnk.com/4ojpq/
Olzak, Tom (2013). TechRepublic. Guidance on business continuity planning, including advice on recovering from natural disasters and man-made disruptive events such as cyberattacks.

[23] *Contingency Planning Guide for Federal Information Systems*
https://xplnk.com/sdy8s/
Also known as SP 800-34. PDF. This is the US National Institute of
Standards and Technology (NIST) document designed to assist organizations in understanding the purpose, process, and format of information
system contingency planning development through practical, real-world
guidelines. It includes a glossary and acronym list.

CISO by Todd Fitzgerald

[24] *CISO Leadership: Essential Principles for Success*
https://xplnk.com/fw5r9/
Fitzgerald, Todd and Micki Krause, editors (2007). Auerbach Publications.
Describes practical, applicable, real-world skills for aspiring senior security
executives.

[25] *Information Security Governance Simplified: From the Boardroom to the
Keyboard*
https://xplnk.com/38fal/
Fitzgerald, Todd (2011). CRC Press. Describes how to implement an information security program.

[26] *Cobit 5 for Information Security*
https://www.isaca.org
Information Systems Audit and Control Association. Practical guidance
for information security.

Confidentiality by Audrey Gendreau

[27] *European Union Data Protection Regulations (EU GDPR)*
https://xplnk.com/7t64m/
European Commission (2016). Summary of the European Union (EU)
General Data Protection Regulation (GDPR) including obligations of
non-European organizations receiving personal data from residents of
the EU.

[28] *Children's Online Privacy Protection Act (COPPA)*
https://xplnk.com/g5s17/
US Law (16 CFR Part 32). Covers how websites and other online services
must handle the collection of information from – and tracking of interactions with – children under 13 years old.

[29] *Personal Information Protection Rules.*
https://xplnk.com/zkqah/
California Code, Civil Code - CIV 1798.83. California rules governing
privacy policies and the handling of personal information of residents to
prevent unauthorized disclosure of their personally-identifiable information to third parties.

[30] *Executive Summary of Review of the Unauthorized Disclosures of Former National Security Agency Contractor Edward Snowden*
https://xplnk.com/xizmt/
US House of Representatives (2016). PDF. Unclassified Congressional report about the Snowden disclosures.

[31] *Guide to Protecting the Confidentiality of Personally Identifiable Information (PII)*
https://xplnk.com/fxq6j/
McCallister, Erika, et al. (2010). NIST SP 800-122. PDF. Guidelines for taking a risk-based approach to protecting the confidentiality of personally identifiable information.

[32] *Biography and brief history of Edward Snowden.*
https://en.wikipedia.org/wiki/Edward_Snowden
Wikipedia. Biography and brief history of Edward Snowden.

Controls by Mark Sears

[33] *NIST SP 800-53 Full Control List*
https://xplnk.com/ixfqq/
US National Institute of Standards and Technology (NIST). This is a complete list of Risk Management Framework (RMF) Security Controls with an assessment of the impact of each control.

[34] *How can you apply Risk Management Framework (RMF) Security Controls to your business.*
https://xplnk.com/tjrkn/
Chief Security Officer. Scholl, Frederick (2017). Review of National Institute of Science and Technology standards and recent improvements designed to align the specifications with private industry requirements.

Dark Web by Chris Vickery

[35] *Hacker Lexicon: What is the Dark Web?*
https://xplnk.com/hhc0u/
Greenberg, Andy (2014). Wired. Introduction to the dark web.

[36] *A More Secure and Anonymous ProPublica Using Tor Hidden Services*
https://xplnk.com/k3lx3/
Tigas, Mike (2016). ProPublica. Why and how ProPublica is using the dark web.

[37] *How the mysterious dark net is going mainstream*
https://xplnk.com/0cvve/
Bartlett, Jamie (2015). TED. Video with transcript. Presentation about the dark web.

Data Leak by Dennis Leber

[38] *Giant Equifax data breach: 143 million people could be affected*
https://xplnk.com/6fda1/
O'Brien, Sara Ashley (2017). CNN Tech.

[39] *The RNC Files: Inside the Largest US Voter Data Leak*
https://xplnk.com/s6nec/
O'Sullivan, Dan (2017). Upguard. Describes the leak of personal information about 198 million US voters.

[40] *Data leak exposed millions of Time Warner Cable customers*
https://xplnk.com/w1vbu/
Fingas, Jon (2017). Engadget.

[41] *Mystery Restaurant Accidentally Leaks Hilarious Notes About Its Guests*
https://xplnk.com/xm3sr/
Morabito, Greg (2017). Eater.com.

[42] *HBO faces hacker threat: pay up, or suffer bigger data leak*
https://xplnk.com/xhkm2/
CBS Moneywatch (2017). CBS/AP.

[43] *Breaking Down HBO's Brutal Month of Hacks*
https://xplnk.com/pxobo/
Barrett, Brian (2017). Wired.

[44] *Why it took more than a week to resolve the huge Verizon data leak*
https://xplnk.com/y4qge/
Schiffer, Alex (2017). Washington Post.

Encryption by John Armstrong

[45] *2017 Ponemon Cost of Data Breach Study*
https://xplnk.com/wnzop/
Ponemon Institute (2017). Research report. Registration required.

Endpoint Security by Michael Dombo

[46] *Why Agencies Need to Protect Their Endpoints, and Not Just Their Networks*
https://xplnk.com/fq6ks/
FedTech Magazine (2017). Discussion of the need for endpoint security and why protecting users from hackers while they use smartphones, tablets, and other mobile devices in the field is critical to secure networks from cybersecurity attacks.

[47] *Report: Companies are wasting massive amounts of money on ineffective security solutions*
https://xplnk.com/5gbn6/
Matteson, Scott (2017). TechRepublic. Insights and costs of insecure endpoints and strategies for protecting systems from cyber threats.

Firewall by Sarah Granger

[48] *The Great Firewall of China*
https://www.greatfirewallofchina.org
Comparatec. Online tool designed to determine whether a website (or other internet content) is available to those who reside in China.

General Data Protection Regulation (GDPR) by Regine Bonneau

[49] *EU General Data Protection Regulation (GPDR) Portal*
http://www.eugdpr.org
European Parliament regulations governing the processing of personal data.

[50] *Data protection reform - Parliament approves new rules fit for the digital era*
https://xplnk.com/84r6l/
European Parliament News. Press Release. Data protection rules designed to give citizens back control of their personal data and create a high, uniform level of data protection across the European Union.

[51] *Preparing for Compliance with the General Data Protection Regulation (GDPR) A Technology Guide for Security Practitioners*
https://xplnk.com/hn5ul/
Wright, Benjamin (2017). PDF. Sans Institute (aka Escal Institute of Advanced Technologies).

[52] *The GDPR Cheat Sheet for Cybersecurity Professionals*
https://xplnk.com/dyyyp/
Mediapro. PDF. Requirements for complying with the European Union General Data Protection Regulation (GDPR), including a discussion of the impacts on business. Registration required.

Hardening by Linda Maepa

[53] *Case Study: Critical Controls that Could Have Prevented Target Breach*
https://xplnk.com/rmiqu/
Radichel, Teri (2014). PDF. Case study about the Target data breach in 2014.

[54] *How a Bunch of Hacked DVR Machines Took Down Twitter and Reddit*
https://xplnk.com/eojo7/
Meyer, Robinson (2016). Describes how lack of hardening of internet-connected devices made it possible to mount a massive Distributed Denial of Service (DDoS) attack.

[55] *Hacker told F.B.I. he made plane fly sideways after cracking entertainment system*
https://xplnk.com/5w6o7/
Barrera, Jorge Barrera (2015). APTN National News.

Identity Management by Evelyn de Souza

[56] *Identity management (ID management)*
https://xplnk.com/qrqmi/
Rouse, Margaret (2017). TechTarget. Discussion of the need for managing digital identities as well as details about the technologies needed to support identity management.

[57] *In the wake of the cyber sprint, OMB to develop new consolidated identity management guidance.*
https://xplnk.com/hizge/
Ogrysko, Nicole (2017). Federal News Radio. Discussion of updated guidelines for US government agencies and contractors issued by the US National Institute of Standards and Technology (NIST) as well as details about the Trump administration's attempt to roll back agency reporting requirements.

[58] *The best identity management advice right now*
https://xplnk.com/m5g1h/
Grimes, Roger A. (2017). CSO Online. The history of identity management and practical advice on reducing risk. Registration required.

Incident Response Plan by M.K. Palmore

[59] *Computer Security Incident Handling Guide (NIST SP 800-61)*
https://xplnk.com/19gwr/
Cichonski, Paul, et al. (2012). National Institute of Standards and Technology (NIST). PDF. Guidelines from the Information Technology Laboratory (ITL) at NIST for incident handling, particularly for analyzing incident-related data and determining the appropriate response to each incident.

[60] *SANS Incident Handlers Handbook*
https://xplnk.com/1ue0q/
Kral, Patrick (2011). Sans Institute (aka Escal Institute of Advanced
Technologies). PDF. Report that provides the basic foundation for IT
professionals and managers to be able to create their own incident response policies, standards, and teams. Includes an incident handler's
checklist (template) designed to help ensure that each of the incident response steps is followed during an incident.

[61] *Recommended Practice: Developing an Industrial Control Systems Cybersecurity Incident Response Capability*
https://xplnk.com/bos3u/
US Dept. of Homeland Security (2009). PDF. Recommendations to help
companies that use industrial control systems prepare for and respond
to a cybersecurity incident.

Insider Threat by Thomas Carey

[62] *Insider Threat Tip Card*
https://xplnk.com/x4142/
US Dept. of Homeland Security (2016). PDF. Best practices for addressing
organizational, behavioral, and technical security issues and mitigating
insider threats.

[63] *Businesses warned of insider cyber threat*
https://xplnk.com/d58g7/
Wallbank, Paul (2017). Financial Review. Discussion of insider threats
and how financial gain, revenge, and desire for recognition drive insiders
to intentionally disclose sensitive or personal information or take malicious actions against the organizations for which they work.

[64] *IT admins gone wild: 5 rogues to watch out for*
https://xplnk.com/xdowo/
Tynan, Dan (2011). InfoWorld. Advice on how to detect rogue insiders
and minimize the damage they can do.

[65] *Data Breach Digest: Perspective is Reality*
https://xplnk.com/0fdxo/
Verizon (2017). PDF. Statistics, metrics, and insight into the who, what,
where, when, and how of data breaches and cybersecurity incidents. The
case study titled "Partner Misuse – the Indignant Mole," is on page 24.

[66] *Exclusive: Poo listed on ham ingredients*
https://xplnk.com/jnj9s/
Disley, Jan (2001). Real-world example of an insider intentionally altering
the content of a luncheon meat product label.

[67] *Washing Instructions On U.S.-Made Bag Apologize For 'Idiot' President*
https://xplnk.com/8no7t/
Papenfuss, Mary (2017). Huffington Post. Real-world example of an insider intentionally altering the care instructions label on a handbag.

Integrity by Daniel Ziesmer

[68] *NIST Special Publication 800-12: An Introduction to Information Security*
https://xplnk.com/x294d/
National Institute of Standards and Technology (NIST) (1995, rev. 2017). US Department of Commerce. PDF. Introduction to information security principles that organizations can use to help understand the needs of their systems.

[69] *Data Integrity in an Era of EHRs, HIEs, and HIPAA: A Health Information Management Perspective*
https://xplnk.com/l4cpo/
Rode, Dan (2012). US Office for Civil Rights, Health and Human Services, National Institute for Standards and Technology Conference. PDF. Presentation slide deck covering confidentiality, integrity, availability, interoperability, standards, and security requirements for healthcare information.

[70] *ISO/IEC 27000:2018. Information technology — Security techniques — Information security management systems — Overview and vocabulary*
https://xplnk.com/cu13k/
ISO (2018). International management systems standards for information security, also known as the Information Security Management System (ISMS) family of standards.

Kill Chain by Simon Puleo

[71] *Killing Advanced Threats in Their Tracks: An Intelligent Approach to Attack Prevention*
https://xplnk.com/nw7tq/
Sager, Tony (2014). PDF. An overview of the steps in the kill chain, including how to detect unknown attacks by integrating intelligence into sensors and management consoles.

Metrics by Keyaan Williams

[72] *NIST Performance Measurement Guide for Information Security*
https://xplnk.com/fr8gq/
Chew, Elizabeth, et al. (2008). National Institute of Standards and Technology (NIST). PDF. A guide to assist in the development of metrics to measure the effectiveness of security controls.

[73] *The Evil of Vanity Metrics*
https://xplnk.com/gvdic/
Jordan, Chris (2017). HelpNet Security. A critique that discusses the need for technical and business metrics in determining the cost of cybersecurity threat prevention and the cost of analyzing and responding to security events.

[74] *How to Measure Anything: Finding the Value of Intangibles in Business*
https://www.amazon.com/dp/1118539273
Hubbard, Douglas W. (3rd ed. 2014). Wiley. Book. Discusses how to measure things often considered "immeasurable," including customer satisfaction, organizational flexibility, technology risk, and technology return on investment.

[75] *Storytelling with Data: A Data Visualization Guide for Business Professionals*
https://www.amazon.com/dp/1119002257
Knaflic, Cole Nussbaumer (2015). Wiley. Book. Covers the fundamentals of data visualization and how to communicate effectively with data.

[76] *Using Security Metrics to Drive Action*
https://xplnk.com/k8kd0/
Tenable Network Security. Recommendations and best practices for communicating with business executives and board members about cybersecurity issues. Registration required.

Multi-factor Authentication by Dovell Bonnett

[77] *Making Passwords Secure - Fixing the Weakest Link in Cybersecurity*
https://xplnk.com/sai5v/
Bonnett, Dovell (2016). Access Smart Media. Book. Debunks many of the myths of infallibility surrounding multi-factor authentication and other high-technology solutions in favor of a pragmatic approach to password management.

[78] *Multi-factor authentication central to helping reduce data breaches: Ostertag*
https://xplnk.com/6tiy2/
Angela Stelmakowich (2017).

[79] *No passwords please: The need of a strong authentication protocol in the digital age*
https://xplnk.com/r5jsv/
Pahuja, Anupam (2017). Moneycontrol. Discusses the importance of strong authentication to prevent identity theft and fraud.

[80] *Practical IT Security for Everyone*
https://youtu.be/TzUV_ygklqg
Lilliestam, Emma (2016). YouTube. Video. Conference talk that provides security tips that are easy to install and use.

[81] *2017 BlackHat Hacker Survey*
https://xplnk.com/2k10s/
Thycotic (2017). Survey of attendees at the 2017 Black Hat Conference in Las Vegas.

[82] *Password Management Evaluation Guide for Businesses*
https://xplnk.com/m0js4/
Keeper Security, Inc. (2017). PDF.

Non-repudiation by John Falkl

[83] *5 Examples of Non-repudiation*
https://xplnk.com/it4to/
Spacey, John (2016). Simplicable Business Guide.

Payment Card Industry Data Security Standard (PCI DSS) by John Elliott

[84] *Payment Card Industry Security Standards Council*
https://www.pcisecuritystandards.org/
PCI Security Standards Council main website.

[85] *Visa guidance on PCI DSS*
https://xplnk.com/udqra/
Visa. Website with information on PCI DSS for merchants who want to work with Visa.

[86] *Mastercard guidance on PCI DSS*
https://xplnk.com/s4dft/
Mastercard. Website with information on PCI DSS for merchants who want to work with Mastercard.

Penetration Testing by Clarence Cromwell

[87] *The Pentagon Opened up to Hackers and Fixed Thousands of Bugs*
https://xplnk.com/cfhw3/
Newman, Lily Hay (2017). Wired. Details about the U.S. Department of Defense bug-bounty project called "Hack the Pentagon" in which the agency offers cash rewards to independent hackers who find and disclose software bugs and other vulnerabilities.

[88] *Eight Myths Not to Believe About Penetration Testing*
https://xplnk.com/0ydkq/
Steinberg, Joseph (2017). Practical advice on adopting and investing in penetration testing. The author dispels several myths about the practice.

[89] *Only do penetration tests if your security program is up to it, say experts*
https://xplnk.com/vgw18/
Solomon, Howard (2016). IT World Canada. Discussion of the importance
of an organization's cybersecurity maturity as a critical success factor in
adopting penetration testing.

[90] *The Penetration Tester Who Your Boss Hires to Hack Your Email*
https://xplnk.com/fijud/
MacMillan, Thomas (2017). New York Magazine. An interview with a
white-hat penetration tester.

Phishing by Jeffrey Rogers

[91] *Hackers target Irish energy networks amid fears of further cyber attacks on
UK's crucial infrastructure*
https://xplnk.com/gqo18/
Dearden, Lizzie (2017). Independent. Investigative report on how a spear
phishing attack targeted senior Irish energy network engineers.

[92] *2016 Enterprise Phishing Susceptibility and Resiliency Report*
https://xplnk.com/g9s41/
Cofense (2016). Examines the factors that lead to successful phishing
campaigns and discusses how empowering employees to report suspected
phishing incidents affects susceptibility. A 2017 version of this report,
which reports similar results, is available at the same website.

[93] *Top 9 Free Phishing Simulators*
https://xplnk.com/0vl80/
InfoSec Institute (2016). Describes several types of phishing simulators
designed to help employees detect possible phishing attacks.

[94] *Phishme Q1 2016 Malware Review*
https://xplnk.com/p4uwq/
PhishMe (2016). PDF. Details malware trends recorded in the first quarter
of 2016 and warns of dramatic increases in encryption ransomware attacks.

[95] *2018 State of the Phish*
https://xplnk.com/djjna/
Wombat Security (2018). An analysis of data from simulated phishing
attacks. Registration required.

[96] *Spear Phishing*
https://xplnk.com/irg9z/
Northcutt, Stephen (2007). Security Laboratory: Methods of Attack Series.

Physical Access Control by Chris Wynn

[97] *Electronic Access Control*
https://www.amazon.com/dp/0123820286
Norman, Thomas L. (2nd ed. 2017). Butterworth-Heinemann. Book.
Covers virtually every aspect of electronic alarm and access control systems and includes insights into the challenges associated with installing, maintaining, and designing them, including valuable information on how to overcome those challenges.

[98] *Effective Physical Security*
https://xplnk.com/28db9/
Fennelly, Lawrence J. (5th ed. 2016). Butterworth-Heinemann. Book.
Covers the latest international standards for risk assessment and risk management, physical security planning, network systems infrastructure, and environmental design.

Policy by Rodney Richardson

[99] *How to Write Policies and Procedures for Your Business*
https://xplnk.com/1a3x4/
WikiHow. Discusses at a high level how to craft written policies and procedures and to provide them in a format accessible to all employees.

[100] *Why Use Plain Language?*
https://xplnk.com/vjts7/
US Government. The Plain Language Action and Information Network (PLAIN) is a group of federal employees from different agencies and specialties who support the use of clear communication in government writing.

Privacy by Jay Beta

[101] *Facebook says data leak hits 87 million users, widening privacy scandal*
https://xplnk.com/k43ep/
Ingram, David (2018). Reuters.

[102] *Is Your Content Safe from Cybercriminals?*
https://xplnk.com/qk3li/
Rosinski, David (2018). Astoria Software.

[103] *Consumer Sentinel Network Data Book 2017: Reported Frauds and Losses by Age, Percentage Reporting a Fraud Loss and Median Loss by Age*
https://xplnk.com/wnnlp/
US Federal Trade Commission (2017). Documents cases of fraud involving financial loss by age group, as reported to the US Federal Trade Commission in 2017. Allows users to view the data at the national level (e.g., median loss from online fraud by age group) and by state (e.g., median loss online fraud by age group in Indiana).

[104] *Cracking the Invulnerability Illusion: Stereotypes, Optimism Bias, and the Way Forward for Marketplace Scam Education*
https://xplnk.com/o9jwq/
Fletcher, Emma and Rubens Pessanha (2016). Institute for Marketplace Trust: Better Business Bureau. PDF. An overview of consumer survey responses collected by the Better Business Bureau in 2016 that show those most likely to be victims of cyber fraud tend to be younger and better educated.

Privilege by Emma Lilliestam

[105] *Principle of least privilege (POLP)*
https://xplnk.com/431zh/
Rouse, Margaret (2008). TechTarget. Discusses the principle of least privilege and its application to restricting access rights for people, systems, software applications, and devices connected to the Internet of Things. Includes video on how to address privileged user access.

[106] *Excess privilege makes companies and data insecure*
https://xplnk.com/60f2x/
Seltzer, Larry (2013). ZDNet. Research results that show most companies do a poor job of managing the permissions and privileges of users on their computers and networks.

[107] *Excessive User Privileges Challenges Enterprise Security: Survey*
https://xplnk.com/vbjak/
Prince, Brian (2015). Security Week. Research results from the "Privilege Gone Wild 2" survey that shows 47 percent of employees say they have elevated privileges not necessary for their roles.

Ransomware by Dave Kartchner

[108] *WannaCry ransomware attack*
https://en.wikipedia.org/wiki/WannaCry_ransomware_attack
Wikipedia. Describes the May 2017 WannaCry ransomware attack and provides details about the attack, the alleged attackers, the response, and the affected organizations.

[109] *Internet Security Threat Report (2017)*
https://xplnk.com/s2car/
Symantec (2017). Digicert. Infographic. Discusses website vulnerabilities, attack types, and covers the estimated costs of responding to cyber attacks.

[110] *Internet Security Threat Report (2018)*
https://xplnk.com/cd839/
Symantec (2018). Report covering known cyberattacks during 2017. Includes useful statistics, infographics, and links to ancillary materials. Registration required.

[111] *2018 Data Breach Investigations Report*
https://xplnk.com/df2y6/
Verizon (2018). PDF. Detailed analysis of 53,000 cybersecurity incidents in 2017, including 2,216 confirmed data breaches.

Regulation by Vanessa Harrison

[112] *The security laws, regulations and guidelines directory*
https://xplnk.com/nwzi4/
CSO Magazine (2012). An international compendium of security laws, regulations, and guidelines with summaries and links to the full text of each law.

Risk Register by Bob Trosper

[113] *Good Enough Risk Register – Template*
https://xplnk.com/uyq63/
Trosper, Bob (2016). Google Spreadsheet. Template for creating a risk register.

Sandboxing by Keirsten Brager

[114] *Understanding the Sandbox Concept of Malware Identification*
https://cwsandbox.org/
The Sandbox. Discusses the need for sandboxes – designated, separate, and restricted environments (or containers) with tight control and permissions – where computer code can run without causing damage.

[115] *2016: Time for Security to Take its Head out of the "Sand" (box)*
https://xplnk.com/67rq5/
Levy, Israel (2016). Infosecurity Magazine. Examines an alternative approach to sandboxing, an endpoint protection approach known as containerization. Discusses the pros and cons of virtual containers as a cybersecurity tool.

Security Awareness by Justin Orcutt

[116] *Knowbe4*
https://www.knowbe4.com/resources
Library of best practices, white papers, and free tools to help those attempting to develop cybersecurity awareness training programs.

[117] *SANS 2017 Security Awareness Report*
https://xplnk.com/otn5x/
SANS Institute (2017). PDF. Registration required.

[118] *NIST Framework Overview*
https://xplnk.com/34wwu/
Amoroso, Edward G. New York University Tandon School of Engineering. Video. An introduction to the NIST framework and to many practical aspects of modern cybersecurity including awareness, compliance, assessments, and risk management. Registration required for the full course on Coursera.

[119] *NIST Cybersecurity Framework Improves Security Awareness*
https://xplnk.com/sm9m7/
Mediapro (2016). PDF. Registration required.

Security Fatigue by Mary Frances Theofanos

[120] *Cybersecurity Fatigue Can Cause Computer Users to Feel Hopeless and Act Recklessly, New Study Suggests*
https://xplnk.com/1ztp4/
National Institute for Standards and Technology. Theofanos, Mary F. (2016). Explores the concept of security fatigue. Argues for the need to develop awareness of the dangers and to help alleviate the fatigue users experience.

[121] *Security Fatigue*
https://xplnk.com/ztjjf/
Stanton, Brian et al. (2016). IT Pro Magazine, 18(5), pp. 26-32. PDF. Identifies the role security fatigue plays in security decisions. Provides three suggestions to minimize security fatigue.

Separation of Duties by Ron LaPedis

[122] *How poor management helped an ABB employee steal $103 million*
https://xplnk.com/6efn7/
Pham, Sherisse (2017). CNN Money. Video. Explores the story of how an employee of a major European company took advantage of lax cybersecurity and disappeared with $103 million of the firm's money.

[123] *Probe of water district finds 'shocking' misuse of public assets*
https://xplnk.com/2awot/
Gutierrez, Melody (2017). SFGate. Story of how lack of oversight allowed employees to allegedly use hundreds of thousands of dollars in public funds for personal purchase.

[124] *2 Top Tyco Executives Charged With $600 Million Fraud Scheme*
https://xplnk.com/rwlyh/
Sorkin, Andrew Ross (2002). New York Times. Story of how executives at Tyco were indicted for allegedly misappropriating $600 million in company funds.

[125] *Former Credit Union Manager, Kathryn Sue Simmerman, Sentenced To Six And A Half Years In Prison For Embezzlement*
https://xplnk.com/9mxhf/
US Department of Justice (2016). Press release. Announcement of Kathryn Sue Simmerman sentence.

[126] *What Every IT Auditor Should Know About Proper Segregation of Incompatible IT Activities*
https://xplnk.com/myyfo/
Singleton, Tommie W. (2012). ISACA Journal, Volume 6, 2012. Discusses the importance of the concept known as separation of duties. Suggests a lack of separation can make it easier for malicious cybercriminals to perform misdeeds undetected.

Shadow Security by Iacovos Kirlappos

[127] *Learning from "Shadow Security": Why understanding noncompliant behaviors provides the basis for effective security.*
https://xplnk.com/n5t8t/
Kirlappos, Iacovos, Simon Parkin, and M. Angela Sasse (2014). Workshop on Usable Security, San Diego, CA. PDF. Proceedings Paper. doi:10.14722/usec.2014.23. Analysis of in-depth interviews with employees of multinational organizations about security noncompliance. Reveals instances in which employees created alternative shadow security mechanisms that allowed them to complete their work and feel like they were working securely, despite not following official policies and procedures. Suggests that lessons learned from shadow security workarounds can be used to create more workable security solutions in the future.

[128] *"Shadow Security" as a tool for the learning organization.*
http://discovery.ucl.ac.uk/1462481
Kirlappos, Iacovos, Simon Parkin, and M. Angela Sasse (2015). ACM SIGCAS Computers and Society, 45 (1), 29-37. PDF. doi:10.1145/2738210.2738216.

[129] *People: the unsung heroes of cyber security*
https://xplnk.com/3nepx/
Jon L. (2017), National Cyber Security Centre. Video. Discusses the need to make cybersecurity *people-centered* in order to defeat cybercriminals. Argues for the importance of exceptional user experiences to help make it easy for employees to comply with cybersecurity guidelines, rules, and regulations.

Situational Awareness by Danyetta Fleming Magana

[130] *Target to Pay $18.5 Million to 47 States in Security Breach Settlement*
https://xplnk.com/77n96/
Abrams, Rachel (2017). The New York Times. Details the $18.5 million settlement Target was ordered to pay as a result of a major data breach that exposed the names, credit card numbers, and other personal information about tens of millions of people in 2013. Includes details on the financial impact the breach had on the popular US-based retailer.

[131] *Anatomy of the Target data breach: Missed opportunities and lessons learned*
https://xplnk.com/fcjwd/
Kassner, Michael (2015). ZDNet. Examines how the Target data breach might have happened and what the retailer could have done to prevent the hack.

[132] *A Practical Guide to Situational Awareness*
https://xplnk.com/fjxo5/
Stewart, Scott (2012). WorldView. Discusses the basics of situational awareness and suggests how to help users develop a cybersecurity mindset (the "right level of awareness") so they can spot threats and report them.

[133] *Why a Long-Term Data Strategy is Essential to Stopping Insider Threats*
https://xplnk.com/7tuqx/
Jackson, William (2017). GovTech Works. Argues for a long-term strategy designed to safeguard personal and other sensitive information that strikes a good balance between access and cost.

Social Engineering by David Shipley

[134] *Social Engineering*
http://www.beauceronsecurity.com/socialengineering
Beauceron Security. Web page with resources and definitions related to social engineering.

[135] *MacEwan University defrauded of $11.8M in online phishing scam*
https://xplnk.com/5i2w9/
Canadian Broadcasting Corporation (2017). Describes how a Canadian university was defrauded of $11.8 million after staffers fell prey to an online phishing scam.

[136] *2016 Data Breach Investigations Report: Executive Summary*
https://xplnk.com/qgbr3/
Verizon (2016). PDF. Detailed analysis of more than 100,000 cybersecurity incidents in 2015, including 2,260 confirmed data breaches in 82 countries.

[137] *Bears in the Midst: Intrusion into the Democratic National Committee*
https://xplnk.com/t0cdt/
Alperovitch, Dmitri (2016). Crowdstrike. Analysis and findings identifying
two separate Russian-intelligence-affiliated adversaries – Cozy Bear and
Fancy Bear – present in the computer network of the US Democratic
National Committee (DNC) in May 2016. Discusses details of the attacks
and provides links to related articles on the subject.

Standards by Ulf Mattsson

[138] *ISO/IEC 2700 family – Information security management systems.*
https://xplnk.com/vvi7c/
International Organization for Standardization (ISO) (2013). Home to
the ISO/IEC 27000 family of standards, which provides a model for setting
up and operating an information security management system.

[139] *Consortium for IT Software Quality (CISQ)*
http://it-cisq.org/
CISQ (2017). IT leadership group that develops international standards
that enable IT and business leaders to measure the risk IT applications
pose to the business, as well as estimate the cost of ownership.

[140] *The ISF Standard of Good Practice for Information Security*
https://xplnk.com/pe6ts/
Information Security Forum (2016). Executive summary of the standard
and information about topics including threat intelligence, risk assessment, security architecture, and enterprise mobility management. Registration required.

[141] *Common Criteria*
http://www.commoncriteriaportal.org/
Home for "Common Criteria for Information Technology Security
Evaluation" and the companion "Common Methodology for Information
Technology Security Evaluation" standards. Common Criteria standards
are used to eliminate redundant evaluation activities, clarify terminology
to reduce misunderstanding, and restructure and refocus evaluation
activities to those areas where security assurance is gained.

[142] *FIPS General Information*
https://xplnk.com/47qkv/
FIPS (2017). National Institute of Standards and Technology (NIST).
Home of US Federal Information Processing Standards that includes a
variety of online resources, publications, and access to a keyword
searchable publication database.

Static Application Security Testing by Lucas von Stockhausen

[143] *BSIMM Framework: Building Security in Maturity Model*
https://www.bsimm.com/
BSIMM. Details of 113 activities performed by mature security initiatives organized into practice areas.

Threat Modeling by John Diamant

[144] *Fundamental Practices for Secure Software Development: A Guide to the Most Effective Secure Development Practices in Use Today*
https://xplnk.com/xj8gp/
Simpson, Stacy, editor (2008). SafeCode. PDF.

[145] *Resilient Security Architecture: A complementary Approach to Reducing Vulnerabilities*
https://xplnk.com/2qqug/
Diamant, John (2011). IEEE Security & Privacy. PDF. Article reprint expanding on the role of threat modeling/analysis. Note that this paper describes a threat analysis example that avoided more than 70 vulnerabilities; since this paper was published, further analysis has increased that number to more than 100. doi:10.1109/MSP.2011.88.

[146] *The New Attack Vector: Applications*
https://xplnk.com/93kmd/
Diamant, John and Jeff Misustin (2017). DXC Technology. PDF. White paper. Describes DXC CATA (Comprehensive Applications Threat Analysis), an example of a robust commercial threat modeling methodology delivered as a service.

Vulnerability Assessment by Jeff Schaffzin

[147] *10-Step Security and Vulnerability Assessment Plan*
https://xplnk.com/shc3x/
ITBusinessEdge (2014). Slide deck. Suggests security and vulnerability assessments be performed against all information systems on a pre-determined, regularly scheduled basis. Recommends third parties be retained periodically to ensure appropriate levels of coverage and oversight. (source: Info-Tech Research Group).

[148] *HIPAA Overview*
https://xplnk.com/8j6kd/
US Department of Health and Human Services (2015). Answers general questions regarding the Standards for Privacy of Individually Identifiable Health Information and the Health Insurance Portability and Accountability Act (HIPAA) of 1996.

[149] *PCI DSS (Payment Card Industry Data Security Standard) Compliance Overview*
https://xplnk.com/0la1a/
TechTarget (2017). Overview of policies and procedures developed to protect credit, debit, and cash card transactions and prevent the misuse of cardholders' personal information.

[150] *GDPR (EU General Data Protection Regulation)*
https://www.eugdpr.org/gdpr-faqs.html
Frequently asked questions regarding GDPR.

Zero-day Vulnerability by James McQuiggan

[151] *'NSA malware' released by Shadow Brokers hacker group*
https://xplnk.com/4xq5x/
BBC News (2017).

[152] *'The ultimate cyberweapon for espionage': The 'Petya' cyberattack is exploiting a powerful NSA tool*
https://xplnk.com/vplul/
Sheth, Sonam (2017). Business Insider. Discusses the Petya cyberattack that exploited a powerful cyberweapon created by the US National Security Agency (NSA).

Contributor Index

Orcutt, Justin, 58

P

Palmore, M.K., 90
Puleo, Simon, 96

R

Richardson, Rodney, 120
Rogers, Jeffrey, 32

S

Schaffzin, Jeff, 84
Sears, Mark, 128
Shipley, David, 14
Shulmistra, Dale, 88
Simchak, Stephen, 56
Stafford, Taylor, 9, 137, 153
Stershic, Kathy, 9, 143, 153

T

Theofanos, Mary Frances, 16
Trosper, Bob, 94

V

Valenzuela, Flavio, 80
Vickery, Chris, 26
von Stockhausen, Lucas, 104

W

Williams, Keyaan, 98
Wynn, Chris, 54

Z

Ziesmer, Daniel, 114

Subject Index

Colophon

About the Book

This book was authored in expeDITA, a DITA-based wiki developed by Don Day. Contents were converted to DocBook, and the book was generated using the DocBook XML stylesheets with XML Press customizations and, for the print edition, the RenderX XEP formatter.

With the exception of this colophon and the advertisement at the back of the book, the interior of this book was generated directly from the wiki with no manual intervention.

About the Content Wrangler Content Strategy Book Series

The Content Wrangler Content Strategy Book Series from XML Press provides content professionals with a road map for success. Each volume provides practical advice, best practices, and lessons learned from the most knowledgeable content strategists and technical communicators in the world. Visit the companion website for more information about the series: contentstrategybooks.com.

We are always looking for ideas for new books in the series. If you have any suggestions or would like to propose a book for the series, send email to proposal@xmlpress.net.

About XML Press

XML Press (xmlpress.net) was founded in 2008 to publish content that helps technical communicators be more effective. Our publications support managers, social media practitioners, technical communicators, and content strategists and the engineers who support their efforts.

Our publications are available through most retailers, and discounted pricing is available for volume purchases for educational or promotional use. For more information, send email to orders@xmlpress.net or call us at (970) 231-3624.

The Content Wrangler Content Strategy Book Series

The Language of Content Strategy

Scott Abel and
Rahel Anne Bailie

Available Now

Print: $19.95
eBook: $16.95

Content Audits and Inventories: A Handbook

Paula Ladenburg Land

Available Now

Print: $24.95
eBook: $19.95

Global Content Strategy: A Primer

Val Swisher

Available Now

Print: $19.95
eBook: $16.95

Author Experience: Bridging the gap between people and technology in content management

Rich Yagodich

Available Now

Print: $24.95
eBook: $19.95

Enterprise Content Strategy: A Project Guide

Kevin P. Nichols

Available Now

Print: $24.95
eBook: $19.95

Intelligent Content: A Primer

Ann Rockley
Charles Cooper
Scott Abel

Available Now

Print: $24.95
eBook: $19.95

The Language of Technical Communication

Ray Gallon

Available Now

Print: $24.95
eBook: $19.95

The Language of Localization

Katherine Brown-Hoekstra

Available Now

Print: $25.95
eBook: $19.95

XMLPress.net